SpringerBriefs in 1

More information about this series at http://www.springer.com/series/10082

Viktor Jakupec

Development Aid—Populism and the End of the Neoliberal Agenda

Springer

Viktor Jakupec
Faculty of Economics and Social Sciences
University of Potsdam
Potsdam
Germany

and

Faculty of Arts and Education
Deakin University
Warrnambool
Australia

ISSN 2211-4548   ISSN 2211-4556 (electronic)
SpringerBriefs in Philosophy
ISBN 978-3-319-72747-9   ISBN 978-3-319-72748-6 (eBook)
https://doi.org/10.1007/978-3-319-72748-6

Library of Congress Control Number: 2017960931

© The Author(s) 2018
This work is subject to copyright. All rights are reserved by the Publisher, whether the whole or part of the material is concerned, specifically the rights of translation, reprinting, reuse of illustrations, recitation, broadcasting, reproduction on microfilms or in any other physical way, and transmission or information storage and retrieval, electronic adaptation, computer software, or by similar or dissimilar methodology now known or hereafter developed.
The use of general descriptive names, registered names, trademarks, service marks, etc. in this publication does not imply, even in the absence of a specific statement, that such names are exempt from the relevant protective laws and regulations and therefore free for general use.
The publisher, the authors and the editors are safe to assume that the advice and information in this book are believed to be true and accurate at the date of publication. Neither the publisher nor the authors or the editors give a warranty, express or implied, with respect to the material contained herein or for any errors or omissions that may have been made. The publisher remains neutral with regard to jurisdictional claims in published maps and institutional affiliations.

This Springer imprint is published by Springer Nature
The registered company is Springer International Publishing AG
The registered company address is: Gewerbestrasse 11, 6330 Cham, Switzerland

Preface

Development aid is a complex and contested concept. It serves as a political tool with the aim to expand or maintain donor countries' geopolitical influences, it is used as a catalyst to improve trade relationships, and it is applied as a measure to impose certain ideological values and norms on aid-recipient countries. Alternatively, it was and is used as a strategy to replace or counteract the existing dominant geopolitical and geoeconomic spheres of interests and ideologies.

In the recent times, a unique geopolitical constellation emerged, namely the rise of populism in Western democracies, the emergence of new development banks and initiatives, and the quest for preserving the existing development aid world order. We have witnessed the electoral success of Donald Trump and his pursuit of populist foreign policies and the development aid agenda. The established Washington Consensus-based International Finance Institutions (IFIs) such as the World Bank, the International Monitory Fund (IMF), the World Trade Organisation (WTO), and other similar institutions defending, promoting, and imposing the dominant neoliberal development aid ideology. The third factor is the emergence of the new development banks dominated by China, such the Asian Infrastructure and Investment Bank (AIIB), the New Development Bank (NDB) formerly known as the BRICS Bank, and the One Belt, One Road (OBOR) initiative.

Trump's populism is challenging the neoliberal ideology of the Washington Consensus institutions (e.g. World Bank, IMF, WTO) and development aid as a political or diplomatic tool. The USA under the Trump administration is retreating from its global development aid leadership role. The China-dominated development banks and initiatives are providing a counterbalance to the neoliberal ideology-based IFIs, by avoiding an imposition of ideological conditionalities on their development aid-seeking countries. This all points to a potential decline of the existing and a rise of new paradigms concerning the future geopolitical development aid world order.

The complexities and contestability of development aid at political and economic levels are further emphasised by the discord amongst the academic community. There is the academic camp referring to the works of William Easterly, Peter Bauer, Milton Friedman, and others which maintains the development aid has been ineffective and inefficient and has failed to deliver the goals of poverty reduction and economic development. There is another camp, claiming the opposite noting the works of Jeffrey Sachs, Joseph Stiglitz, Nicholas Stern, amongst many others. Academic discourse which does not subscribe to the claims of negative and positive impacts, efficiencies and effectiveness of development aid is limited.

Much of the academic discourse is focussed on issues concerning the dominant development aid ideology, namely neoliberalism, and claims that there is insufficient evidence to show that the existing Washington Consensus neoliberalism has advanced the economic or political well-being of developing nations globally. Of course, there are successes, but many are not well documented, and much of development aid outcomes and impacts are shrouded in secrecy.

Conceptualising and Defining Development Aid

Having outlined very briefly the current events concerning development aid, we can now turn to the concept of development aid in more detail. For a better understanding a working definition of development aid may be in place. It is often referred in the literature, social media and political discussion as foreign aid, international aid, or foreign assistance. The most commonly accepted definition was formulated by the Development Assistance Commission (DAC) of the Organisation for Economic Cooperation and Development (OECD), which specifies development aid as a flow of finances or commodities, and provision of technical assistance to developing countries with the aim to promote economic development including social welfare (e.g. health and education). It excludes military aid and humanitarian and emergency aid, and is in a form of grants or subsidised loans (OECD 1972; Radelet 2006).

Drawing on traditional delineations, for the purpose of this discussion, the following development aid definition will be used, namely development aid denotes

...voluntary transfer of public resources from a government to another independent government, to a Non-Government Organisation or to an international organisation (such as the World Bank or the UN Development Program) with at least a 25% grant element, one goal of which is to better the human condition in the country receiving aid (Lancaster 2007, p.9)

To clarify, development aid as defined above promotes technical assistance, financial flows, and trade, with the purpose to advance economic development and social welfare and is afforded as subsidised loans or grants.

Preface vii

Setting the Scene

It is evident from the above definitions that development aid is mainly considered an economic activity. As it was identified above, it also fulfils a political purpose. The latter is, however, missing in the above-stated definitions. However, even a brief perusal of the literature concerning development aid shows that development aid is claimed not only as a component of economics (e.g. development economics) but also as part of the political sciences (e.g. international relations and international studies). Discussions and analyses of development aid may also be found in social sciences, anthropology, social policy, human geography and socio-legal studies, and other cross-disciplinary studies.

It may be tempting to pursue development aid narrative within a framework of competing ideologies, and economic and political orientations. However, such an undertaking is beyond the scope of this discussion. This assessment of the sociopolitical and socio-economic aspects of development aid will be firmly couched in the discipline called 'development studies', rather than economics or political sciences. In this context, development studies is seen as a multidisciplinary sub-discipline of social sciences including aspects of politics and economics.

Book Focus

This book focusses on the potential impact of Trump's economic agenda on the Washington Consensus-based development aid. The point of departure is the recognition that the Washington Consensus has been and still is the politico-economic cornerstone of global development aid. However, since the USA presidential election in 2016, the future of the Washington Consensus has been put in question by the Trump administration. To restate, the neoliberal ideology that dominates the thinking and practices of the Bretton Woods institutions is under attack by the populist movement.

Due to the very character of populism, it is not surprising that Trump's economic rhetoric including development aid is subject to much academic commentary and analyses. Neither is it surprising that the economists are divided and uncertain how to classify Trumponomics. The criticism ranges from Trumponomics being based on isolationism, protectionism, antiglobalisation, anti-neoliberalism—terms used in a negative sense, mainly by proponents of neoliberalism, who have the stoutest vested interests in the protection and continuation of the existing political and economic establishment. Others dismiss Trumponomics uncritically by labelling it as nationalist, isolationist, and protectionist.

A generally acceptable definition of Trumponomics, beyond that it is a multiplicity of economic policies which the Trump administration is attempting to implement under the 'America First' doctrine, is wanting. Thus, perhaps a more constructive understanding of Trumponomics and its effects on development aid may be achieved by taking a step back and subject Trump's populist rhetoric to a critical analysis.

Content and Structure

The content of this book is organised into self-contained chapters. This allows the reader to choose the reading sequence. Each chapter focusses on specific aspects of populism and development aid and the reader may concentrate on some in preference to other chapters. Despite the self-contained content, the chapters together provide a compelling critical analysis of populism and its effect on development aid.

Chapter 1: The Rise of Populism
Drawing on the recent political developments in Europe and the USA and the public discourse since 2016, an analysis of the rise of populism on the left and the right is articulated and it provides an understanding of the contemporary populist political landscape. This includes an analysis of the Trump phenomenon and his type of populism within a context of Trump's foreign policy and development aid. This is contrasted with the neoliberal view couched in Fukuyama's 'End of History' theorem and the rejections of the political elites and the establishment in Western democracies.

Chapter 2: Development Aid—An Historic-Political Overview
Development aid is an important catalyst for economic development and international politics since the end of WWII. This chapter provides a discussion and a critical analysis of the main political, social, and economic developments in development aid. It traces the development agenda from the advent of the Bretton Woods agreement and the Truman Doctrine and the Marshall Plan, to the Washington Consensus and its neoliberal manifesto. The failure of Washington Consensus and the rise of the post-Washington Consensus is analysed and provides a backdrop for the critique of economic globalisation as a development aid cornerstone.

Chapter 3: A Critique of the Development Aid Discourse
This chapter offers a critical review and analyses of the development aid academic and institutional discourse. Some major shortcomings concerning development aid are articulated, including the dominance of economics at the expense of politics, and the imposition of development aid neoliberal conditionalities which act as barriers to socio-economic development in aid-recipient countries. In conclusion, development aid is recast as an inference that it needs to be reconciled within critical frameworks of different sides of the political spectrum.

Preface   ix

Chapter 4: Trumponomics
This chapter provides a deconstruction of the Trump's foreign policy vision and
Trumponomics. It is shown that Trump projects a vision without much ideology but
arguably a vision with sufficient potential for pragmatism and *Realpolitik*. This
deconstruction is based on an articulation of the theoretical and conceptual
frameworks including philosophical, political, and economic perspectives, and the
mercantilist groundings. In conclusion, it is argued that Trumponomics contrasts
with the 'transformational diplomacy' of previous US administrations. Instead, it is
immersed in short-sighted 'transactional diplomacy', which will have a significant
impact on the values of development aid.

Chapter 5: The Potential Impact of Trumponomics on Development Aid
The main discussion in this chapter focusses on megatrends and scenarios. The
former are the overarching tendencies in social, political, and economic environments, which may affect development aid in a context of donor and recipient
countries. The latter provide an outline of potential actions that the Trump
administration will implement. The megatrends refer to (1) transition from globalisation to de-globalisation and (2) transition from neoliberal 'Aid for Trade' to
mercantilist 'Trade not Aid'. The scenarios provide an outline of (1) Trumponomics
and the development aid diplomacy and (2) Trumponomics, the Beijing Consensus,
and the future of development aid.

Potsdam, Germany   Viktor Jakupec

References

Lancaster, C. 2007. *Foreign aid: Diplomacy, development, domestic politics.* Chicago and
    London: Chicago University Press.
OECD (Organisation of Economic Cooperation and Development). 1972. *Official development
    assistance—definitions and coverage.* Paris: OECD.
Radelet, S. 2006. *A Primer on Foreign Aid—Working Paper No. 92.* Washington, DC: The Center
    for Global Development.

Contents

1 The Rise of Populism 1
  Introduction 1
  Understanding the Contemporary Political Landscape 6
  The Trump Phenomenon 7
    Trump's Populism 8
  Trump, Foreign Policy and Development Aid 9
    Trump, Sanders and Economic Populism 9
  From 'End of History' to 'Post-end of History' 10
  The Rejection of the Political Establishment 12
  Conclusion 14
  References 15

2 Development Aid—An Historic-Political Overview 19
  Introduction 19
  The Bretton Woods Agreement and the Truman Era 21
    The Bretton Woods Agreement 21
    The Marshall Plan 22
    The Truman Doctrine 23
    The Truman Point Four Programme 24
  The Washington Consensus Epoch as a Neoliberal Manifesto 25
  The Failure of the Washington Consensus and the Rise
  of the Post-Washington Consensus 27
  Economic Globalisation as a Development Aid Cornerstone 29
  Conclusion 31
  References 32

3 A Critique of the Development Aid Discourse 37

Introduction 37

The Development Aid Discourse 38

A Critical Review of the Development Aid Discourse............ 39

Conditionalities as Barriers to Socio-economic Development........ 43

The Political Economy—Bringing Politics Back into Development

Aid Economics.. 46

Recasting Development Aid—An Inference 48

References 48

4 Trumponomics 53

Introduction 53

Towards a Theoretical Framework of Trumponomics 55

Populism Restated Within a Theoretical Framework 57

Towards a Conceptual Framework of Trumponomics 57

Trumponomics: Philosophical Perspectives.................... 58

Trumponomics: Political Perspectives....................... 60

Trumponomics: Economic Perspectives 60

The Mercantilist Turn of Trumponomics 61

Dismantling the Neoliberal Manifesto of the Washington

Consensus 63

Concluding Thoughts 64

References 65

5 The Potential Impact of Trumponomics on Development Aid...... 69

Introduction 69

Megatrend: Transition from Globalisation to De-globalisation 71

Megatrend: From Neoliberal Aid-for-Trade to Mercantilist

Trade-not-Aid.. 73

Scenario: Trumponomics and the Development Aid Diplomacy........ 75

Scenario: Trumponomics, the Beijing Consensus and the Future

of Development Aid 78

Conclusion 81

References 83

About the Author

Professor Viktor Jakupec is an academic at Deakin University, Australia, and the University of Potsdam, Germany. His research background is in development studies and politics of education. He holds a Dr. phil. from FU Hagen, and a M.Ed. (1st Hons) from James Cook University. He held academic positions at the University of Technology, Sydney, and Deakin University, Australia, and Adjunct Associate Professorships at the Queensland University of Technology, Australia, and the University of South Australia. His recent publications include *Trumponomics: From Foreign Trade to Foreign Aid*; *Development Aid: Regulatory Impact Assessment and Conditionality*; *The Relevance of Asian Development Bank: Existing in the Shadow of the Asian Infrastructure Investment Bank*; and the co-edited book *Assessing the Impact of Foreign Aid: Value for Money and Aid for Trade*. He worked as an international consultant on World Bank, International Finance Corporation, Asian Development Bank, Millennium Challenge Corporation, EU, European Training Foundation, and bilateral agencies funded development aid projects in Asia, MENA, and the Balkans.

Abbreviations

ADB	Asian Development Bank
AfD	Aktion für Deutschland (Action for Germany) party
AfDB	African Development Bank
AfT	Aid for Trade
AIIB	Asian Infrastructure Investment Bank
ANO	Action of Dissatisfied Citizens party (*Akce nespokojených občanů*)
DAC	Development Assistance Committee of the OECD
EBRD	European Bank for Reconstruction and Development
EMC	European Monetary Crisis
FIDESZ	Fiatal Demokraták Szövetsége, (Alliance of Young Democrats, Hungary)
FN	Front National (National Front) Party, France
FPÖ	Freiheitliche Partei Österreichs (Freedoms Party, Austria)
GFC	Global Financial Crisis
IFI	International Finance Institution
IMF	International Monetary Fund
JICA	Japan International Cooperation Agency
KORUS	United States-Korea Free Trade Agreement
MCC	Millennium Challenge Corporation
NAFTA	North American Free Trade Agreement
NDB	New Development Bank (also known as BRICS Bank)
NGO	Non-Government Organisation
OBOR	One Belt, One Road Initiative
ODA	Official Development Assistance
OECD	Organisation of Economic Cooperation and Development
ÖVP	(Österreichische Volks Partei) Austrian Peoples Party
PEA	Political Economy Analyses
PiS	Prawo i Sprawiedliwość (Law and Justice) party, Poland
Podemos	'We can' political party, Spain
PRS	Poverty Reduction Strategy

PVV	Partij voor de Vrijheid (Party for Freedom), Netherlands
SAL	Structural Adjustment Lending
SPÖ	Sozialdemocratische Partei Österreichs (Austrian Social Democrat party)
SYRIZA	Synaspismós Rizospastikís Aristerás party, Greece
TnA	Trade not Aid
TPPA	Trans-Pacific Partnership Agreement
TTIP	Transatlantic Trade and Investment Partnership
USA	United States of America
USAID	United States Agency for International Development
USSR	Union of the Soviet Socialist Republics
WTO	World Trade Organisation

Chapter 1
The Rise of Populism

Abstract Drawing on the recent political developments in Europe and the USA, and the public discourse since 2016, an analysis of the rise of populism on the left and the right is articulated with the aim to provide an understanding of the contemporary populist political landscape. The Trump phenomenon and his form of populism is analysed within the context of foreign policy and development aid. This is contrasted with the neoliberal view couched in Fukuyama's 'End of History' theorem, and the current popular sentiment towards anti-establishment and anti-globalisation in Western democracies.

Keywords Populism · Trump phenomenon · Development aid
End of history · Foreign policy · Political establishment

Introduction

Brexit and the Trump presidency have dominated much of the public discourse since 2016, and continue to do so. Following closely was the election of the populist right-wing Party for Freedom in the Netherlands, and Le Pen's success in the first round of the French presidential election in 2017. These political events may arguably be seen as manifestations of the rise of right-wing populism, which may have flow-on effects in other countries. However, there are also signs of the rise of left-wing populist movements, as demonstrated by the electoral support for Corbyn's Labour Party populist policies in the 2017 UK parliamentary election.

With the rise of populism in Western democracies, be it left-wing or right-wing, we are witnessing a profound and fervent politically hostile response to existing political, social and cultural values. This applies not only to domestic but equally to foreign policies. The latter, however, play a significant role in defining the outcome of development aid. The most pertinent contemporary and globally far-reaching example of the rise of populism is the election of Trump as the president of the USA. While the Trump phenomenon mirrors what's happened elsewhere, the USA being the largest global economy and the single largest contributor to development

© The Author(s) 2018
V. Jakupec, *Development Aid—Populism and the End of the Neoliberal Agenda*,
SpringerBriefs in Philosophy, https://doi.org/10.1007/978-3-319-72748-6_1

aid (OECD 2017) it may be reasonable to argue that it will have the single most significant impact on development aid globally. Thus, in order to understand the impact of Trump's populist foreign policies concerning development trajectory it is necessary to view it through a lens of political events and changes.

From this vantage point, development aid is governed by geopolitical interests, political expedience, and economic ideologies. Carothers and De Gramont (2013, p. 3) point out historically that foreign aid, 'has had an uncertain and uncomfortable relationship with politics'. Such relations and governance may become even more discomforting due to major political changes witnessed in 2016. Indeed, 2016 may be remembered as the defining moment for an ideological and political change in the Western liberal democracies with voters' rejection of the UK's membership of the EU (Brexit) and the electoral success of Donald Trump. Both events herald a success for national populism as a political movement and lend moral and political support to the rise of similar political movements in Europe (cf. Judis 2016).

In the 2017 general election in the Netherlands, the populist PVV led by Wilders became the second largest party in the Dutch parliament. It holds 20 seats, an increase of five seats. Wilders and the PVV did not form a government, nor did it join the governing coalition. However, PVV ideas might be taken up by other parties. In other words, Wilders may be credited for moving Dutch politics to the right, especially as far as immigration is concerned. This shows that the populist right and far right parties do not need to be in government to influence the political agenda.

In France's 2017 presidential election, the populist National Front candidate, Marine Le Pen defeated candidates from the socialists and conservative parties whose presidential nominees have prevailed for 60 years. Although Le Pen lost in the run-up election against a centralist newcomer, Emmanuel Macron, she has been successful in putting her 'France First' message across to millions of voters, especially in the adversely affected northern Rust Belt.

Despite Le Pen's unsuccessful bid for the presidency, she and her party have changed France's political landscape. Macron, has moved to the right of centre and adopted some populist policies in order to win the parliamentary support he needs to realise his election promises. Not dissimilar to Trump, he has portrayed himself as being outside the political establishment and has built his own political movement.

Setting aside the populist characteristics of being outside the main political parties, Macron exhibits some other populist predispositions. In his election campaigns, he proclaimed the need for a new brand of politics, he argued for the reforms of the European Union, and he made it clear that his is not a political party on the right or the left, but a movement. Of course, this is not the 'strong' populism propagated by his opponent Le Pen or that of Trump (cf. Sheridan 2017). Macron, in his inauguration speech promised to give the French back the confidence in themselves and France's future, to restore France's global standing, and to reform and relaunch the EU. He promised to shake up France's political order and bolster France's economy. This is not too far from Trump's rhetoric to make 'America great again', to 'drain the swamp' to 'renegotiate trade treaties' and to protect USA industries.

Introduction 3

Perhaps the most overt populist inclination displayed by Macron was at the argument he presented to the summit of the European heads of states in Brussels on 23rd June 2017. He argued for 'une Europe qui protège'—a protective Europe. He argued that only when the European Union can prove that it can protect its citizen from the consequences of globalisation and unrestrained trade will the Eurosceptics and populists be restrained (Kafsack 2017). Following his ascent to the French presidency, Macron announced that the French voters expect a profound political transformation, including a reduction of the number of parliamentarians and their terms, and to speed up the legislative processes by using his presidential powers. This is a 'soft' populism, a homoeopathic therapy to the 'hard' populism; Macron is heralding non-conforming non-populist populism.

In the UK, Theresa May took up a populist cause in the form of 'hard' Brexit. However, it is debatable to what extent May will diverge from Trump's and Le Pen's protectionist policies. It should be noted however, that Brexit was won on the premise of UK regaining control of immigration and reclaiming national sovereignty from the EU and its institutions. The electoral success of the Labour Party under Corbyn's leadership in UK with its left-wing populist policies has similar political manifestos to those articulated by Trump and Sanders. For example, Corbyn in his election campaign addressed issues concerning the former industrial areas which previously offered employment in coal mines, power stations, manufacturing plants, and are now the equivalent to the USA Rust Belt.

In New Zealand's 2017 parliamentary election the populist-nationalist New Zealand First Party won the third largest number of seats. The two largest parties, namely the National and the Labour party, respectively, even with their traditional coalition partners, cannot form a majority government. Thus, the populist New Zealand First Party will decide which major party will form a coalition government. This, of course, means that whichever major party forms the coalition with the New Zealand First Party, must accept certain populist-nationalist policies.

In the 2017 German federal election (*Bundestagwahlen*), the established parties, i.e. the centre right CDU party and its CSU sister party, and the centre left Social Democrat SPD lost seats to the far-right populist Aktion für Deutschland (AfD) party. The electoral success of the AfD is significant, for a number of reasons. One, the AfD is now the third strongest party and second largest opposition party. Two, the AfD popular vote rose from 4.7% in the 2013 federal election to 12.6% in 2017. Also notable is the fact that there has been no far right party in Germany's federal parliament since 1961.

The results of the Austrian federal election (*Nationalratswahlen*) in October 2017 show a significant move towards far-right populism. The centre right Austrian Peoples Party (ÖVP), under the leadership of the Eurosceptic populist Sebastian Kunz became with 31.47% the biggest party, followed by the Austrian Social Democratic Party (SPÖ) with 26.86% of votes and the Austria's Freedom Party (FPÖ) with 25.97%. The FPÖ gained 5.46%, the populist ÖVP 7.48% and the SPÖ gained 0.04%. However, it should be noted that Austria has a political history of nationalism and nativism and it could be argued that the 2017 elections is a Renaissance of the political shift towards populism on the far right.

Also in October 2017, the populist far-right Action of Dissatisfied Citizens party (*Akce nespokojených občanů* ANO) movement led by Andrej Babis has decisively won the Czech Republic's legislative election in a vote that shifted the country to far-right populism and paved the way for the Eurosceptic movement to lead the country. ANO with 29.7% of votes has decisively defeated the country's traditional political centralist and conservative parties, almost three times as much as any other party. Notably' ANO is the first party since the demise of Communist era, 25 years to abolish the political domination of two mainstream centre-right and centre-left parties.

The recent rise of extreme right populist AfD in Germany the FPÖ in Austria and the ANO in the Czech Republic is not dissimilar to other European countries, such as Hungary, Poland, and Slovakia, where a significant number of the electorate voted for far-right parties that promise protection of national economic, and nationalist cultural and social values. These sentiments and policies are articulated by populist leaders through simple everyday utterances, giving an impression of presenting truth. They project dramatized views about national priorities and domestic needs and articulate the grievances of sections of the population that might feel disenfranchised. The disenfranchisement is expressed through the ordinary peoples'

> ...deep cynicism and resentment of existing authorities, whether big business, big banks, multinational corporations, media pundits, elected politicians and government officials, intellectual elites and scientific experts, and the arrogant and privileged rich (Inglehart and Norris 2016, p. 6).

The key problem for development aid in a populist or national populist environment is not the lack of funding, but a failure to demonstrate that it brings benefits to the donor nation, including more employment for the disenfranchised population. Politicians, political scientists, development economists and agencies, aid practitioners, International Finance Institutions, (IFIs) and NGOs have, to a large extent, failed to provide a pragmatic explanation for this situation—thus giving credence to the populist critique. One reason for this failure may well be the perception among the political elite and other vested interests who propagate the infallibility of neoliberal ideology. However, a cautionary note may be in place here because neoliberalism is an ambiguous and '...an oft-invoked but ill-defined concept' (Mudge 2008, p. 703).

While not wanting to oversimplify neoliberalism, it may be defined in a broad sense as

> ...a political strategy that seeks to make as much of our lives as possible conform to the economist's ideal of a free market. That simple idea is all one really needs to understand what it is about, and it has been the ruling idea of most governments in the western world and beyond for almost 40 years (Crouch 2017, p. 8)

From a politico-economic ideology vantage point it advocates free-market economy, unfettered free trade, economic and financial deregulation, competition, privatisation, political agendas of class rule, and imposition of fiscal austerity to reduce the government involvement in economic matters as advocated, for example by Hayek (2001), Friedman (2002) and others.

To be sure, the scholarly literature on neoliberalism is overwhelming, both as sympathetic and critical discourse. Some of the discussions which unpacks neoliberalism at epistemic and pragmatic levels may be found in works of Cahill and Konings (2017), Crouch (2011, 2017), Mirowski (2014), Streeck (2014, 2016), Jones (2012), Harvey (2005) and many others.

Returning to the writings of Hayek and Freedman, neoliberalism may be defined as

> ...a political strategy that seeks to make as much of our lives as possible conform to the economist's ideal of a free market. That simple idea is all one really needs to understand what it is about, and it has been the ruling idea of most governments in the western world and beyond for almost 40 years (Crouch 2017, p. 8).

To clarify, following from the liberal tradition of Adam Smith, Hayek's philosophy is couched the 'minimal state' theorem and the basic critique of the social justice concept. The 'minimal state' condition, according to Hayek, is a means to escape from the rule of the middle class that governs the political process aiming to redistribute wealth trough public institutions.

To put its differently, the 'minimal state' condition is the foundation of neoliberalism, and

> Neoliberals regard government as a particularly incompetent institution, the less of which we have, the better. The market is seen as self correcting in a way that is more flexible and responsive than anything that can be achieved by government regulation (Crouch 2017, p. 11).

Of course, from this vantage point it is possible to interpret Hayek and Freedman as opposing development aid through IFIs, especially the IMF and the World Bank, for both are 'state-like' organisations. Thus, developing countries would benefit from escaping from the rule of the IFIs that govern the political process with the aim aiming to redistribute wealth as a public institution.

However, it is problematic to justify the 'minimal state' concept in accordance with neoliberal ideology to disenfranchised voters. The 'minimal state' theorem opens the path to deep globalisation and thus reinforces the rise of populism as seen in the election in a number of EU countries and the USA. This requires due to the populist notion of nativism a better understanding of the potential impact of national populism on development aid which requires a paradigmatic political and economic shift. We need to step back and unpack the contemporary political landscape; look beyond the Trump phenomenon and the retreat of the neoliberal dogma embedded in Frances Fukuyama's 'End of History' thesis (Fukuyama 1989, 1992) and then outline the populist rejection of the political establishment and elite. This approach has the potential to contextualise a background aiming to analyse the impact of national populism on development aid.

Understanding the Contemporary Political Landscape

Following the election of Donald Trump as the 45th President of the USA, the development community and organisations find themselves in unchartered waters. There is general unease among the development studies community, including development economists, sociologists, political scientists and practitioners. Trump's policy details are vague, and potentially the Trump administration will refocus existing development policies within a strategy that supports 'America First' and 'Make America Great Again'.

Throughout the campaign, Trump maintained that he does not want to provide development aid to countries that 'hate' the US (Fiske 2017). He also committed to invest in domestic infrastructure projects in lieu of other countries (Grimley 2016). This would not be significant except that, as noted above, the US is the single largest contributor to development globally and changes to development aid funding will affect aid donor agencies and aid recipient countries.

Furthermore, it appears that the Trump administration will subordinate development aid to foreign trade policies. This is in line with the recognition by the development aid community that historically, foreign trade policies are central to policy formulation of development (Krueger 1997); and as Tarnoff and Nowels (2005) explain, development aid is a primary, 'component of the international affairs budget and is viewed by many as an essential instrument of U.S. foreign policy' (p. 1). From this perspective, there is a nexus between foreign policies and development aid.

Consequently, any fundamental changes in foreign relations and trade policies will have a corresponding change in foreign aid. Furthermore, with the rise of populism, and especially nationalist populism, conventional (neoliberal) thinking about development aid may not be valid for much longer. To further explain these changes, this chapter will analyse the rise of the national populism in Western democracies with a special focus on the Trump Phenomenon. It proposes that the so-called 'End of History' theorem articulated by Fukuyama has not come to fruition and that Trump's nationalist populism has emerged as new ideology in competition with post-Cold War neoliberalism. One of the hallmarks of the newly emerged populist phenomenon is the rejection of the political establishment to embrace nationalist interests.

This chapter will analyse the reasons for protests against the political establishment, focussing on unfulfilled neoliberal promises of a 'better world'. It will include an analysis of the Trump phenomenon from both the neoliberal right and the socialist left, by illustrating the commonalities between Trump's and Bernie Sander's political rhetoric.

The rise of populism as an ideological counter movement to neoliberalism is further analysed by contrasting Fukuyama's assertions that east-west ideological battles are over and that liberal democracy with neoliberal ideology had triumphed, leading to the 'End of History'. The relevant point is that the Fukuyama doctrine has been uncritically accepted by most, if not all, IFIs including IMF, the World

Bank, the Asian Development Bank (ADB), the European Bank for Reconstruction and Development (EBRD), The African Development Bank (AfDB), as well as many bilateral funding agencies, including USAID and the Millennium Challenge Corporation (MCC) among others. However, Fukuyama's theorem can be described as an unfinished project as a new ideological battle has emerged, namely the populist and anti-neoliberal capitalist versus the neoliberal capitalist ideology.

In conclusion, the potential reasons for populist rejections of neoliberalism, with its free-market ideology, are canvassed. Neoliberalism is put into a context of being the 'End of History'—a governing philosophy embraced globally by the post-Soviet Union political elite and Western democracies. The analysis will focus on Trump's rhetoric purging Washington of the 'establishment', thus capturing the imagination and the popular wrath of a certain group of voters.

The Trump Phenomenon

To understand the Trump Phenomenon, one must recognise that he expressed an interest to stand for the presidency as early as 1988 (Kruse 2016). It would be wrong to assume he came from nowhere. It took him some 30 years to fulfil his ambition, nevertheless, his success in 2016 surprised the political elite and the establishment on both sides of the US political spectrum, as well as other parts of the world. The question posed by political analysts, academics, commentators and politicians is simple: why Trump? The literature thus far seems to support two theses. First, certain socio-economic groups, especially poor, white males without a college degree in the US (Thompson 2016) feel disenfranchised. They are angry with the establishment and the political elite because over the past 40 years living standards have either stagnated for the lower middle-class workers or declined for the low-wage earners (Mishel et al. 2015). Similar situations exist in EU member countries (World Economic Forum 2017).

Second, the public in Western democracies does not seem to trust politicians, political parties and what they represent. These two theses are mutually inclusive. In relation to the first thesis, Trump captured this anger and responded with a rhetoric that gave the socio-economically disadvantaged hope. He went on to proclaim that the US must come first and that he will rebuild the US to achieve new economic success. As far as the second thesis is concerned, Trump did not come from the political elite or the establishment. If anything, he portrayed himself, and was accepted by a significant number of the population, as being determinedly anti-political elite and establishment. This found resonance, especially among the lower socio-economic strata of the population who were experiencing high unemployment and rising inequality due to low economic growth. He also successfully linked the notion of economic growth with the anti-political elite establishment by rejecting economic and military globalisation in favour of the national interest (Seidel and Chandy 2016).

Building on the established literature, the main issues that gave rise to the Trump phenomenon was his recognition of the following: (1) general hostility among the lower economic social strata towards the establishment and elites who are perceived to pursue policies to benefit corporations and the wealthy; (2) A establishment support for globalisation which has seen the relocation of manufacturing industries to less developed countries and an increased struggle for jobs at the lower end of the skill base; (3) a consequent loss of trust by the poorly educated working class; And (4) the political establishment's failure to comprehend the consequences of the rise of populism.

So how was the Trump phenomenon born? This is a socio-economic and political question. The literature attempts to answer the question by referring to broader socio-economic issues, especially to the 'new normal' of unemployment and underemployment, stagnating or regressing wages, and corporate relocation. However, these circumstances also existed during the previous election cycle. Trump might have brought into focus a discussion concerning unemployment, globalisation and other social issues in the US, but he does not have a monopoly on the discussion.

Trump's Populism

Most scholarly literature claims populism is associated with the political right and far right (Mudde 2017; Berlet and Lyons 2000; Betz 1993). There is evidence to the contrary. Indeed, much of the populist movement is located on the right of the political spectrum and this is not a purely USA phenomenon. There is also populism on the right and the left of the political spectrum. For example, on the right and far right we can find the United Kingdom Independence Party, the National Front (FN) in France, Aktion für Deutschland (AfD) in Germany, the Party for Freedom (PVV) in the Netherlands, Austria's Freedom Party (FPÖ), the Action of Dissatisfied Citizens (ANO) party, the One Nation Party in Australia, the FIDESZ Party in Hungary, the Law and Justice Party (PiS) in Poland and the New Zealand First party. On the left of the political spectrum are the Five Star Movement in Italy, Podemos in Spain, and Syriza in Greece. Some of these parties have been more successful than others in forming a government. But there are strong indicators that the balance of power in Europe and other Western countries is changing in favour of populism (Moffitt 2016; Judis 2016).

It could be argued that Trump is neither a right-wing nor a left-wing populist, but has adopted, policies from both sides of the political spectrum. Furthermore, it is noteworthy that the rise of populism and the demise of the neoliberal ideology was not an abrupt event. It was not caused by Trump, but has happened incrementally at least since the onset of the GFC and further fuelled by the ongoing European Monetary Crisis (EMC). Populism on both sides of the political spectrum is a reaction against the political elite which maintains the neoliberal economic agenda, especially globalisation. The political elites over-guaranteed and under-delivered on globalisation (Milanovic 2016; Stiglitz 2002). Recognising the failure of the elite, it is not surprising that Trump disassociated himself from the bi-partisan consensus held by elites and the Washington establishment on issues of international trade, foreign policy and immigration.

Trump, Foreign Policy and Development Aid

In his election campaign, Trump advocated and pursued a complete change of direction in US foreign trade policies. His criticism of US neoliberal globalised foreign trade reflects the sentiments of a significant number of the population. However, he has thus far not articulated a coherent alternative policy and his utterances are, with some notable exceptions, often contradictory. Trump's neoliberal establishment critics are questioning his ability to offer a better option to free trade (Ötsch and Pühringer 2017; Fraser 2017). As the election results show, Trump's insight into lower socio-economic perceptions of foreign trade, at least from certain electoral colleges, are often accurate. Trump argues for nationalism and protectionism within a political framework of strategic independence. This is in contrast with the US establishment elite which advocates internationalism and neoliberalism.

Trump, Sanders and Economic Populism

Trump does not fit into the traditional Republican nor the traditional Democratic political camp. Potentially, he is outside the two-party political establishment, for he adopted both left and right populist policies. As indicated above, there are parallels between the political position taken by Sanders and those exhibited by Trump. Sanders exploits economic populism in a similar way to Trump and both oppose economic globalisation. A typical example is the rejection of the Trans Pacific Partnership Agreement (TPPA), with a view to rebuff other international trade agreements. On the domestic front, both are in favour of sustaining or increasing existing levels of social security benefits and tax increases on some wealthy groups (Ball 2016).

Both, Trump and Sanders campaigned against 'the rigged economy' and 'the rigged political system' that has supported and protected an economy, which is detrimental to the USA domestic interest. Both reject the duplicitous influence of money in politics and share the conviction that the money spent on the wars in the Middle East, especially Iraq, would be better utilised for domestic infrastructure investment (Kuttner 2016). Both support single-payer health care, and have concerns about increased immigration quotas (Naylor-Komyatte 2016).

Trump and Sanders have similar policies regarding higher education. Trump argues the government should not profit from student loans. He maintains loan repayments should continue, but without profit-taking. Accordingly, higher education is an investment in the country's future. This may well be perceived as the view that higher education is a public good, rather than a private commodity (Sullivan 2015). In the same vein, Sanders argues that student loan interest rates should be massively reduced and that the government should not profit from student loans (DuVall 2016). He believes that investing in an educated workforce makes a country more competitive in today's global economy. Again, this is a reconfirmation that education must be a public good, rather than a private commodity.

Of course, there are serious differences between Sanders' and Trump's policies, which are beyond the scope of this discussion. However, the populists on both sides of the political spectrum may be right in advocating protectionism, as the neoliberal free-market politicians have completely underestimated the negative effects of global trade on the lower economic and the poorly educated social strata. Politicians and the establishment have failed to lift the living standards of the economic losers. They together with the elites too often assume neoliberalism as a default setting,

It is apparent the Trump, by addressing the economically disadvantaged and condemning the establishment and the elite has raised the discourse of neoliberal globalisation versus nationalist protectionism at political as well as academic levels. He has brought to the fore the potential end of the Fukuyamian 'End of History' doctrine, embraced by the neoliberal political elite and the establishment in most Western democracies. His support came from Republicans and others, be it from the left or the right, who have lost their belief in government.

From 'End of History' to 'Post-end of History'

Trump's electoral success comes at times when the Western democracies were secure in their belief of the infallibility of the neoliberal economic system, which has been in place since the end of the Cold War. This is reflected in Fukuyama's (1989, 1992) 'End of History' theorem. To restate, Fukuyama simply claimed that the neoliberalism has triumphed over the Soviet-style communist ideology and there were no viable alternatives to former and free-market philosophies espoused by Hayek (2001) and Friedman (2002). This arguably produced a false security among the Western political elite, for not many political leaders envisaged the unprecedented success of the populism, and especially the Trump Phenomenon. There are two points to consider. Firstly, the 'End of History' theorem received much support from neoliberal politicians including Ronald Reagan and Margaret Thatcher. Both embraced Hayek's and Friedman's theses on free-market led economy. The same applies to contemporary US politicians like Paul Ryan and Ted Cruz. For them the Fukuyamian 'End of History' theorem holds true.

However, in an unambiguous juxtaposition to the Republican Party leadership Trump does not see himself as a neoliberalist but as a populist on the basis that he represents the people with the aim to 'make deals' which benefit the American populace. This is partially, and for the time being, correct. In reality, however, the potential risk is that these deals may represent the theories of Hayek and Friedman and reinforce Fukuyama's 'End of History' and the neoliberal agenda. Here we should remember that '[n]eo-liberalism is not the natural human condition, it is not supernatural it can be challenged … because its own failures will require this' (George 2001, n.p). With that in mind, there is a potential for the Trump administration to turn neoliberal and revalidate the Fukuyamian 'End of History' theorem.

The assertion that neoliberalism and Western democracy were the apogee of human political development and could and would not be surpassed is the bedrock of Fukuyama's thesis. It gave rise to the political dogma that there is no other alternative. Suspicions of the disenfranchised voters that the political elite might not be interested in changing people's lives were reinforced. Fukuyama's 'End of History' theorem failed in its sustainability.

Given the unprecedented quick collapse of the Soviet empire Frances Fukuyama's assertions that the East–West ideological battles are over and that the liberal democracy and capitalism of the West had triumphed, seemed plausible. Fukuyama's message was simple: totalitarianism, authoritarianism, and communism are once and forever finished And the economic and political neoliberalism are the victors. The future belongs exclusively to Western democracy and free-market economy, which surmount all economic, political and social contradictions. Therefore, the war of ideologies has ended.

Fukuyama was as wrong as all of the philosophers of history who thought they could interpret the future. On balance, the rise of populism is neither an end of history nor the end of ideologies; it is the end of the Fukuyamian 'End of History'. With the demise of the Soviet Union and the Marxist socialist ideology on the political world stage, neither the Hegelian notion of the liberal state nor the Marxian concept of communism has been achieved.

Fukuyama and his neoliberal disciples' basic mistake was to believe that the victory of the neoliberal order meant the end of all and every ideology. Unfortunately, for Fukuyama, ideology is an anthropological constant. We may have witnessed the demise of the ideological battle between capitalism and socialism or communism, but a new battle has emerged, namely the populist and anti-neoliberal capitalist versus the pro-neoliberal capitalist ideology.

In all fairness, Fukuyama did peruse the options of the potential rise of nationalism and religious fundamentalism, but dismissed them as unlikely events to succeed. Thus, the victory of neoliberalism was prospectively lasting. As it was stated above, a number of European countries are moving towards nationalism (e.g., France, The Netherlands, Great Britain, Hungary, Poland and others) and the USA under Trump administration is also moving in this direction. Furthermore, Fukuyama was right in one sense. He envisaged a political system where the conventional ideologies no longer impacted on voters, whereby the population would be able to take part in issue-based political decisions.

It should be acknowledged that the political elite was often unable to reconcile their policy platforms with the ideological and pragmatic limitations imposed upon them by global institutions and agencies such as the WTO, IMF, World Bank and others pursuing the removal of trade barriers and trade agreement. These limitations were, and still are, outside the formal electoral forums a phenomenon that became increasingly acute since the rise of neoliberalism as the only viable ideology. Through globalisation, international and domestic trade policies became interdependent. The relationship between neoliberalism and globalisation is not a new phenomenon. Globalisation and the 'End of History' theorem have ultimately widened the scope of foreign policies on trade and subsequently development aid (Severino and Ray 2010; Hynes and Scott 2013). This has led to globalisation dogma becoming increasingly more relevant domestically, especially as it applies to foreign policies relating to development aid—no longer a domain reserved for the national political establishment. It has become a decision-making sphere of the global political elite.

Globalisation politics were fused with domestic national policies, which subsequently impact on policy responses. The national governments found it difficult to offer answers couched in national interests, which are reflective of the needs of the population. The disenfranchised sections of the population feel exposed to increased global complexities. They either retreat from politics or search for apparent simple political answers and solutions and align themselves with political movements that are providing an anti-elite and anti-establishment policy platforms. Mainstream parties on the right and the left, find it increasingly difficult to reconcile their domestic versus global policies and thus their governing credibility. They find their policies being vanquished by populist challenges, which, in turn, facilitated a collapse in the popular belief of Fukuyama's 'End of History' theorem and the global neoliberal agenda. The elite was unable to convince working and lower middle classes that the neoliberal ideology will bring economic prosperity not only for the elite and the global economy but also for the working classes.

Since the late 1980s the neoliberal international order that signified the end of history has failed to enable the working class in the rich developed and industrialised countries to achieve the higher living standards they expected. It was after all this failure that provided support for Trump's populist movement in the USA. He advocated the Marxian redistribution of wealth for the poor on the one side and the protection of wealth for the rich on the other side. Both the redistribution and protection are to ensure that the economic policies work for everyone. Are we witnessing the beginning of a new history, or is history repeating itself?

The Rejection of the Political Establishment

In order to understand the underpinnings for the rejection of the political establishment and elites by the lower socio-economic sections of populations in the Western democracies, it is important to note that after the end of the Cold War, political parties on the left and right have been reshaped. This may well be one of the reasons for the subsequent rise of populism with its rejection of the political establishment, for the centre-left and centre-right became two sides of the same coin. The right has adopted political platforms that mirror those of the left, whereby the latter shifted increasingly to the centre. On many levels, the centre right and centre-left economic policies became indistinguishable. This brought to the fore two occurrences that for a while supported the 'End of History' theorem. One took on the characteristics of neoliberalism akin to Angela Merkel's ordoliberalism (van Esch 2014) with its leanings towards managerialism and technocracies. The other is based on national identity with a focus on hostility towards immigration. In today's' political environment it is Trump in the USA, Le Pen on the right and Melenchon on the far-left Parti de Gauche in France who align their reactionary politics to economic and social policies previously ascribed to the left: protection of employment, welfare state support and opposition to austerity. Thus, it is not surprising that the working class, which traditionally voted for parties on the left have abandoned the ideals of such parties termed as the New Left and are shifting their support towards the populist movements and policies with the hope to regain their place and status in national politics and economics (Kriesi 2010).

We have identified in the preceding discussion. The question is, what do the left and far-left as well as right and far right populist parties have in common and where are the differences? For example, Syriza and Podemos parties stand against the establishment, globalisation, and austerity, whereas The Five Star Movement is against the establishment, the Eurozone and austerity. The FPÖ is against the establishment, globalisation, the European Union, the Eurozone, immigration, and Islam. The PVV is against the establishment, the European Union, the Eurozone, immigration, and Islam. The FN is against the establishment, globalisation, the European Union, the Eurozone, immigration, and Islam. AfD party is against the establishment, the Eurozone, immigration, and Islam. The UK Independence Party is against the establishment, globalisation, the European Union, the Eurozone, and immigration.

To summarise: (1) all of the above cited populist parties on the left and the right are anti-establishment; (2) all of the cited left or far-left parties are against austerity, which indicates against some aspects of neoliberalism; (3) Podemos and Syriza on the political left and UK Independence Party, FN and FPÖ on the right or far right share anti-globalisation policies and programs; (4) all of the right-wing parties, except AfDand the French Parti de Gauche are against the European Union; and (5) all of the above populist parties on the right are anti-immigration and anti-Islam. It is evident that there are significant commonalities for populist parties on the right and the left, foremost anti-establishment and globalisation (Ashkenas and Aisch 2016).

The question is how did this political paradigm shift happen? On the surface, the working classes across Europe, the USA and other parts of the Western world are protesting against a political system, which they do not see as acknowledging them. They do not see themselves as being part of a society with which they can identify. Trump recognised this sentiment amongst the working class and poorly educated lower middle classes, by posing the rhetorical question: 'Vote for me—what do you have to lose?' In essence, Trump recognised the possibility that with years of little or no discernible economic benefit emerging from the existing political and economic structures, why not demolish it and see what happens?

This had a certain appeal for those who have lost their conventional means through which to voice their frustrations with and the feeling of disfranchisement from the political establishment. They see themselves as neglected equally by the centre-left and the centre-right. Thus, the working class and lower middle class, feeling politically and economically marginalised by the elite have turned to identity politics (Coate and Thiel 2010; Evans and Tilley 2017; Wiarda 2014). It could also be argued that the marginalisation is potentially a cultural identity loss. The deterioration of the political and economic influence of working and lower middle class through the decline of the labour organisations and the weakening of social democratic parties have helped to disguise the political and economic foundations of social problems. Thus, cultural identity became the vehicle through which social, economic and political issues are deflected, and the language of national identity emerged as the populist voice of discontent. It is not as one may assume the identity policies of the left, it is the identity policies of the right. It is the politics of nationalism, social, cultural and economic protectionism that provide the groundswell for many populist movements.

A significant section of the population in Western countries is resisting an economy perceived as devaluing their work and labour. These people are rebelling against a political culture they see as devaluing their previous secure place in the society. They resent what they see as the drastic socio-cultural changes from without. In short, there is economic anxiety, racial resentment, ennui, misogyny and a movement against the elite that represent these threats.

Conclusion

In this chapter, we identified and discussed a number of concepts and issues, all within a context of populism, ranging from the Trump phenomenon to the neoliberal notions embedded in Fukuyama's 'End of History' theorem, to the rejections of the political establishment by working and middle classes in the Western democracies. These concepts are linked together by a 'red thread,' and an overarching theme, namely hostility towards elites, established global institutions, and mainstream political parties of the Western democracies. Populism has taken the mantra of being the voice of forgotten ordinary people and a voice of authentic national interests, which by its own definition rejects globalisation. It is also evident that populist parties and politicians are located on the left as well as on the right of the political spectrum. Under normal circumstances, this left-right alignment would cause a certain amount of political ambiguity. But populism has developed a 'new normal' political singularity which is reinforcing political ambiguity. Nor does it articulate a new social, political or economic order. Instead, everything is adjudicated regarding specific axiological idiosyncrasies.

Over the past years, populist parties have won government in Greece, Hungary, Italy, Poland, Czech Republic, and Austria, and have formed a government with other parties in Finland, Lithuania, and Norway. In USA and Philippines populist leaders portray themselves as political strongmen and became presidents. They are perceived by the disenfranchised and poorly educated population as a higher authority with a mission to restore the one-time social, cultural and economic order. Notwithstanding this perception and the rise of the anti-establishment populism, the neoliberal political elite have shown a lack of willingness to reconstruct an end of the 'End of History' political and economic agenda.

The populist parties are on the rise in the West; among voters the right-wing populists are achieving consistent support, while the left-wing populist parties have sporadic support (Caccavello 2017; Heinö 2017). Over the past few years, some 70 million Europeans have elected populist parties in their most recent parliamentary elections. This is equivalent to approximately 22% of voters throughout Europe. As it stands populists, on the right and the left, have positioned themselves as the third-strong political parties in Europe. In nine European countries, seven of which are EU countries, populist parties are part of the government and thus historically have unprecedented political power. As Heinö (2017) points out, the growing rejection of globalisation, immigration and refugees, EU integration and multiculturalism as a factor of mobilisation for the right-wing populists, provides a fertile ground for a slow but steady growth of right-wing populist movement. Given the current upsurge in voter support for the populist movement, populism does not appear to be a passing phenomenon, as it is based on structural causes.

It is important to note that development aid has been and still is a part of foreign policy and diplomacy and thus an instrument of statecraft. However, with the rise of globalisation, it became subject to structural power arrangements in the global economic system. This led to elitist view and populist view about development aid, respectively. The populist ideals projected by the Trump's foreign policy point towards drastic changes concerning development aid. Trump administration and most likely other populist parties in Europe will redefine development aid in the image of another 'new world order' perhaps moving away from the foreign policies of economic globalisation. The development aid agenda which over the past two decades went beyond narrowly defined national interests may well turn its back on economic globalisation interests.

References

Ashkenas, J., and G. Aisch. 2016. European Populism in the Age of Donald Trump. *The New York Times*, (December 5, 2016). https://www.nytimes.com/interactive/2016/12/05/world/europe/populism-in-age-of-trump.html. Accessed February 2, 2017.

Ball, M. 2016. What Trump and Sanders have in common. *The Atlantic*, (n. p.). https://www.theatlantic.com/notes/2016/01/what-bernie-sanders-and-donald-trump-have-in-common/422907/. Accessed March 30, 2017.

Berlet, C., and M.N. Lyons. 2000. *Right-Wing Populism in America*. New York: The Guilford Press.

Betz, H.-G. 1993. The New Politics of Resentment: Radical Right-Wing Populist Parties in Western Europe. *Comparative Politics* 25 (4): 413–427.

Caccavello, G. 2017. TIMBRO Authoritarian Populism Index 2017: A Summary. *Epicenter-European Policy Information Center*. https://timbro.se/app/uploads/2017/07/briefing-timbro-authoritarian-populism-index-2017.pdf. Accessed July 12, 2017.

Cahill, D., and M. Konings. 2017. *Neoliberalism*. Cambridge: Polity.

Carothers, T., and D. De Gramont. 2013. *Development Aid Confronts Politics: The Almost Revolution*. Washington/Moscow/Beijing/Brussels: Carnegie Endowment for International Peace.

Coate, R.A., and M. Thiel. 2010. *Identity Politics in the Age of Globalisation*. Boulder, CO: First Forum Press.

Crouch, C. 2011. *The Strange Non-Death of Neoliberalism*. Cambridge: Polity.

Crouch, C. 2017. *Can Neoliberalism be Saved from Itself?*. London: Social Europe Ltd.

DuVall, E. 2016. On the issues: Student loan reform offers rare moment of agreement for candidates. *UPI News*. http://www.upi.com/Top_News/US/2016/05/26/On-the-issues-Student-loan-reform-offers-rare-moment-of-agreement-for-candidates/7681463777489/. Accessed March 2017.

Evans, G., and J. Tilley. 2017. *The New Politics of Class: The Political Exclusion of the British Working Class*. Oxford: Oxford University Press.

Fiske, A. 2017. Why Trump Cutting U.S Foreign Aid Could Make Amerika Less Safe. *UPROXX News* (February 27, 2017). http://uproxx.com/news/donald-trump-foreign-aid-policy/. Accessed March 2017.

Fraser, N. 2017. Progressive Neoliberalism versus Reactionary Populism: A Choice that Feminists Should Refuse. *NORA* 24 (4): 281–284.

Friedman, M. 2002. *Capitalism and Freedom*, 14th Anniversary ed. Chicago: The University of Chicago Press.

Fukuyama, F. 1989. The end of history? *The National Interest* 16: 3–18.

Fukuyama, F. 1992. *The End of History and the Last Man*. London: Penguin Group.

George, S. 2001. A short story of neo-liberalism: twenty years of elite economics and emerging opportunities for structural change. *Socioeco* (February 2001). (n.p.). http://www.socioeco.org/bdf_fiche-document-1007_en.html. Accessed February 14, 2017.

Grimley, N. 2016. Will Trump embrace the funding of overseas aid? *BBC News* (December 20, 2016). http://www.bbc.com/news/world-us-canada-38334846. Accessed March 1, 2017.

Harvey, D. 2005. *A Brief History of Neoliberalism*. Oxford: Oxford University Press.

Hayek, F.A. 2001. *The Road to Serfdom*. London/New York: Routledge.

Heinö, A.J. 2017. Timbro Authoritarian Populism Index 2017—Briefing Paper. *Timbro*. https://timbro.se/ideologi/timbro-authoritarian-populism-index-2017-2/. Accessed July 12, 2017.

Hynes, W., and S. Scott. 2013. *The Evolution of Official Development Assistance: Achievements, Criticisms and a Way Forward*. OECD Development Co-operation Working Papers No. 12. Paris: OECD Publishing.

Inglehart, R.F., and P. Norris. 2016. *Trump, Brexit and the Rise of Populism: Economic Have-Nots and Cultural Backlash*. Faculty Research Working Paper, John F. Kennedy School of Government. Cambridge MA: Harvard University.

Jones, D.S. 2012. *Masters of the Universe: Hayek, Friedman, and the Birth of Neoliberal Politics*. Princeton: Princeton University Press.

Judis, J.B. 2016. *The Populist Explosion: How the Great Recession Transformed American and European Politics*. New York: Columbia Global Reports.

Kafsack, H. 2017. Macron scheitert mit Vorstoß für Investitionskontrolle. *Frankfurter Allgemeine Zeitung* (July 24, 2017). http://www.faz.net/aktuell/wirtschaft/wirtschaftspolitik/gipfeltreffen-in-bruessel-macron-scheitert-mit-vorstoss-fuer-investitionskontrolle-15074574.html. Accessed July 24, 2017.

References

Kriesi, H. 2010. Restructuration of Partisan Politics and the Emergence of a New Cleavage Based on Values. *West European Politics* 33 (3): 673–685.

Krueger, A.O. 1997. Trade Policy and Economic Development: How We Learn. *NBER Working Paper No. 5896* (January 1997). http://www.nber.org/papers/w5896. Accessed February 2, 2017.

Kruse, M. 2016. The True Story of Donald Trump's First Campaign speech-in 1987. *Politico Magazine* (February 5, 2016). http://www.politico.com/magazine/story/2016/02/donald-trump-first-campaign-speech-new-hampshire-1987-213595. Accessed February 10, 2017.

Kuttner, R. 2016. Sanders, Trump and Economic Populism. *The American Prospect* (January 12, 2016). http://prospect.org/article/sanders-trump-and-economic-populism. Accessed February 10, 2017.

Milanovic, B. 2016. *Global Inequality: A New Approach for the Age of Globalization*. Cambridge, MA: Belknap Press.

Mirowski, P. 2014. *Never Let a Serious Crisis Go to Waste*. London: Verso.

Mishel, L., E. Gould, and J. Bovens. 2015. Wage Stagnation in Nine Charts. *Economic Policy Institute* (January 6, 2015). http://www.epi.org/publication/charting-wage-stagnation/. Accessed March 1, 2017.

Moffitt, B. 2016. *The global Rise of Populism: Performance, Political Style, and Representation*. Palo Alto: Stanford University Press.

Mudde, C. 2017. *The populist radical right—A reader*. Milton Park: Routledge.

Mudge, S. 2008. What is Neo-liberalism? *Socio-Economic Review* 6 (4): 703–731.

Naylor-Komyatte, M. 2016. Populism for Plutocrats: How Trump Co-Opted the Sanders Approach. *Brown Political Review* (March 11, 2016). http://www.brownpoliticalreview.org/2016/03/populism-for-plutocrats-how-trump-co-opted-the-sanders-approach/. Accessed January 20, 2017.

OECD. 2017. Net ODA (indicator). *OECD*. https://doi.org/10.1787/33346549-en.

Ötsch, W.O., and S. Pühringer. 2017. *Right-wind populism and market-fundamentalism: Two mutually reinforcing threats to democracy in the 21st century*. ICAE Working Paper Series—No. 59. Linz: Institute for Comprehensive Analysis of the Economy, Johannes Kepler University.

Seidel B., and L. Chandy. 2016. Donald Trump and the future of globalization. *Brookings Up Front*. https://www.brookings.edu/blog/up-front/2016/11/18/donald-trump-and-the-future-of-globalization/. Accessed February 17, 2017.

Severino, J.-M., and O. Ray. 2010. *The End of ODA (II): The Birth of Hypercollective Action*. Working Paper 218, (June 2010), Washington, DC: Center for Global Development.

Sheridan, G. 2017. French Election: Emmanuel Macron's new twist on populism. *The Australian* (April 29, 2017). http://www.theaustralian.com.au/opinion/columnists/greg-sheridan/french-election-emmanuel-macrons-new-twist-on-populism/news-story/7802d3ee24730a4cb681392c09d92058. Accessed January 19, 2017.

Stiglitz, J. 2002. *Globalization and its Discontent*. New York: W. W. Norton & Company Inc.

Streeck, W. 2014. *Buying Time*. London: Verso.

Streeck, W. 2016. *How Will Capitalism End?*. London: Verso.

Sullivan, M. 2015. Bernie Sanders on Education: 5 Things the Presidential Candidate Wants You To Know. *Forbes Education* (April 30, 2015). http://www.forbes.com/sites/maureensullivan/2015/04/30/bernie-sanders-on-education-5-things-the-presidential-candidate-wants-you-to-know/#71b52f0c2fcb. Accessed January 19, 2017.

Tarnoff, C., and L. Nowels. 2005. *Foreign Aid: An Introductory Overview of the U.S. Programs and Policies*. Washington: CRS Report for Congress.

Thompson, D. 2016. Who are Donald Trump's Supporters Really? *The Atlantic* (March 1, 2016). https://www.theatlantic.com/politics/archive/2016/03/who-are-donald-trumps-supporters-really/471714/. Accessed March 2017.

van Esch, F. 2014. A Matter of Personality? Stability and Change in EU Leaders' Beliefs during the Euro Crisis. In *Making Public Policy Decisions: Expertise, Skills and Experience*, ed. D. Alexander, and J. Lewis, 53–72. London: Routledge.

Wiarda, H.J. 2014. *Political Culture, Political Science, and Identity Politics: An Uneasy Alliance*. Farnham: Ashgate Publishing Limited.

World Economic Forum. 2017. Decline in living standards in advanced countries highlights need for new model. Davos: World Economic Forum. http://www.cnbcafrica.com/insights/special-reports/world-economic-forum/wef-davos-2017/2017/01/18/weak-and-unequal-recovery-five-year-average-decline-in-living-standards-in-advanced-countries-highlights-need-for-new-growth-model/#. Accessed February 17, 2017.

Chapter 2
Development Aid—An Historic-Political Overview

Abstract Development aid has been an important catalyst for economic development and international politics since the end of WWII. A critical analysis of the main political, social and economic advances in development aid, traces the development agenda from the advent of the Bretton Woods agreement, the Truman Doctrine and the Marshall Plan, to the Washington Consensus and its neoliberal manifesto. The failure of the Washington Consensus and the rise of the post-Washington Consensus is analysed providing a backdrop for the critique of economic globalisation as a development aid cornerstone. Trump's rejection of the neoliberal globalisation agenda and departure from post-WWII ideologies is discussed.

Keywords Bretton woods · Truman doctrine · Washington consensus
Development aid · Neoliberalism · Populism · Globalisation

Introduction

Political ideologies and foreign policies of the Western countries have been at the centre of foreign aid ever since colonialization in the 19th century. The ideologies and policies changed over time. Foreign aid was perceived as facilitating the economic growth of developing countries, strengthening the geopolitical influence of the donor country, or providing aid that supports peoples' basic human needs. Of course, these three are not mutually exclusive.

It was not until the end of WWII that development aid was constituted on an international scale rather than by bilateral arrangement. The former has maintained some influence until today. This discussion will commence with the post-WWII development aid and cover historical-political epochs to the present.

Our discussion of the historical-political overview of development aid is structured as follows: (i) the Bretton Woods Agreement, the Marshall Plan and the Truman Doctrine Epoch; (ii) the epoch covering the Washington Consensus as a neoliberal manifesto of development aid; and (iii) the epoch characterised by the

---

© The Author(s) 2018
V. Jakupec, *Development Aid—Populism and the End of the Neoliberal Agenda*,
SpringerBriefs in Philosophy, https://doi.org/10.1007/978-3-319-72748-6_2

failure of the Washington Consensus and the rise of the post-Washington Consensus. The chapter will focus on the concept of globalisation, which is perceived by right-wing populist movements as a cornerstone of the neoliberal ideology. Within this is the notion that globalisation disadvantages the lower socio-economic population and advances the interests of the political elite and the establishment.

Throughout these epochs the economic and political focus of development aid changed in many respects, such as from the Keynesian economics to neoliberal economics of Friedman and Hayek to an elusive post-neoliberalism paradigm and populist response to the failure of the Washington Consensus in foreign aid. Some background to development aid offers context for these three eras.

Foreign aid, as we know it, is a relative new political and economic concept. Economists such as Smith, Ricardo, Stuart Mill and Marx did not pay much attention to foreign aid. There was a general view that colonies would level with the developed countries through trade and export. In terms of the political background, one of the first legislation concerning official aid was the Colonial Development Act passed in 1929 by the UK Parliament (Abbott 1971) and the Colonial Development and Welfare Act in 1940 and 1945 (Overseas Development Institute 1964).

In the USA, the first legislation addressing foreign aid was the European Recovery Program, also known as the Marshall Plan, which was enacted in 1948 (Gimbel 1976). Noteworthy from a historic-political vantage point is the Harry Truman inaugural presidential 'Four Point Speech' delivered on 20th January 1949. He advanced the idea that foreign aid to underdeveloped nations is a vital component of USA foreign policy; indeed, the economic advancement of underdeveloped nations was a key component of Truman's administration (Ekbladh 2010).

The next milestone at international policy level was the establishment of the Development Assistance Group within OECD in 1960, which was reconstituted in 1961 as DAC. In the same year legislation was passed in various countries in support of development aid. This includes the establishment of the Kuwait Fund for Arab Economic Development, Germany's Kreditanstalt für Wiederaufbau (KfW), Japan's Overseas Economic Cooperation Fund, Sweden's Agency for International Assistance (since 1965 Swedish International Development Authority) and USAID. In subsequent years, other countries join DAC (2006).

Throughout the 1950s and 1960s development aid policies were mainly focussed on big capital-intensive projects, paying little attention to policies, programs and projects linked to employment, human capital, labour and productivity. In the late 1960s and early 1970s this changed and the neoclassical model of economic growth was adopted. Development aid policies focussed on basic needs. During the 1980s and the 1990s, development aid became increasingly dependent on the recipient country's willingness to adopt a neoliberal market economy, including privatisation, decentralisation and removal of trade barriers (Edwards 2014; Williams 2011; Morgenthau 1962). The early 2000s have seen the emergence of new development banks, such as Asian Infrastructure Investment Bank (AIIB) and the New Development Bank (NDB), focussing mainly on infrastructure (Jakupec and Kelly 2015). This has required a modified international development aid political position

Introduction 21

from the traditional IFIs and donor governments in relation to foreign policy and foreign aid strategies. Since 2011, a new factor has emerged within the development aid agenda, namely its linkage to the war on terror. Issues regarding human rights, anti-corruption, environment protection became standard loan conditionalities of the traditional agencies, but not necessarily of the new aid agencies (Figaj 2010; Lebovic and Voeten 2009).

The Bretton Woods Agreement and the Truman Era

Historically the Bretton Woods Agreement, the Marshall Plan, the Truman Doctrine and the Truman Point Four Plan occurred at about the same time, namely between 1944 and 1949. These were in response to the reconstruction of Europe and the establishment of the USA geopolitical supremacy, (vis. the Soviet Union). Economic considerations were, to a large extent, subordinated to political objectives. Historically and politically the Bretton Woods Agreement, the Marshall Plan and the Truman Doctrine are closely related.

The Bretton Woods Agreement

The Bretton Woods agreement refers to the international monetary system that predominated from the end of World War II until the early 1970s. The agreement is based on the outcome of the 1944 held conference at Bretton Woods, New Hampshire. The discussion was, to a large extent, dominated by John Maynard Keynes economic theory. As far as development aid is concerned one of the important events emerging from the conference was the agreement to establish the IMF and the World Bank. The IMF was formally established in December 1945. The World Bank group evolved from a single institution in 1944 to an incorporation of five development organisations (Peet 2009).

The IMF was charged with the responsibility to provide reserve currencies loans to countries, and to monitor exchange rates. The World Bank was given the function to provide financial assistance to nations during the post WWII reconstruction era. USA became the major contributor to both IFIs, which in turn led to USA hegemony of the development aid, by providing long-term loans through the Marshall Plan as well as other aid programs.

From a political perspective, the Bretton Woods Agreement was based on liberalism with the aim to extract from the participating nations a commitment to accept liberal multilateralism and the newly emerging interventionist economic systems, which became globally prominent during the 1930s (Ikenberry 1993). Over time and not surprisingly, the Bretton Woods Agreement attracted its share of criticism. Arguably one of the more persistent and widely accepted criticisms concerns the Bretton Woods institutions' approach to international development. In much of the literature the Bretton Woods Agreement is seen as an outcome of the Anglo-American talks during 1942 and 1944. In these negotiations neither country gave much attention the needs of the poorer, mainly 'southern' developing and impoverished countries (Helleiner 2014). Thus, it was suggested by critics of the Bretton Woods Agreement that the system imposed by the Bretton Woods institutions has over many years advantaged the rich Western aid-donor countries at the expense of the poor developing aid-recipient nations. The Bretton Woods Agreement was suspended and subsequently dissolved between 1968 and 1973.

The Marshall Plan

Named after the then US Secretary of State, George C. Marshall, the Marshall Plan was submitted by President Truman to the Congress in December 1947. However, it was not until April 1948 that he signed the bill initiating the European Recovery Program (as the Marshall Plan was officially named). Over the first three years the Marshall Plan distributed in excess of USD 12 billion in USA aid to 16 European countries (Hogan 1987). In addition to the targeted aid, the Marshall Plan also provided funding for a Technical Assistance Program, enabling engineers, technical experts and industrialists from European countries to visit USA with the purpose to gain first-hand experience of USA industrial capitalism and to facilitate technology transfer. Conversely, USA experts went to Europe as advisors to provide technical assistance in support of industrial development. Arguably, the Marshall Plan, as measured by the GDP of recipient countries was a success. At a political level, the Marshall Plan prevented the spread of communism and became a basis for European integration (Gillingham 2003). It helped to advance European economic growth in the immediate post-WWII era (Burk 2001).

Overall, the Marshall Plan was more a political than an economic instrument. However, Western governments needed both political and economic help. This served both the political and national interests of the USA and the economic needs of Western governments (Lundestad 2003). In developing and implementing a political and economic nexus the USA accepted individual and tractable policies amongst the Western European governments. Nevertheless, through the Marshall Plan the USA was able to structure the overall political environment within these countries in a manner that realised its foreign policy goals (McGlinchey 2009). This included the geopolitical containment of the Soviet Union and the establishment of permanent USA military bases throughout Western Europe, preventing the far-left socialist, fascist and communist parties gaining political control in Western European countries (Lundestad 2003).

The Marshall Plan is undeniably connected with the policy of restraining the Soviet Union. As a political agenda, its potential to manifest the European East-West conflict cannot be understated (Cromwell 1979). Combined, the Truman Doctrine and the Marshall Plan merged two well-defined opposing politico-economic sides—Western capitalism on the one side and Soviet-style communism on the other. Thus, both the Marshall Plan and the Truman Doctrine may be perceived as two sides of a coin designed to counteract Soviet expansion. The Marshall Plan on its own was a central model of the explicit exploitation of economic power in the USA foreign policy (Burk 2001).

In 1953 the Marshall Plan formally ended. Foreign aid moved away from capital and technical assistance of the Marshall Plan and shifted focus towards basic human needs, such as education, health, food and nutrition, human resource development and population planning (Wood 1986). The Marshall Plan was more than simply an economic stimulus package or even a structural adjustment program instilling free-market values and institutions into Western Europe (Magid 2012). The Marshall Plan served as a lead up to the formation of the European Union and Marshall's vision provides important guidelines for today's development aid political agendas. Agendas to speed-up economic development globally, commencing with the retreating from the ideologies of the Washington Consensus and its effects on the economies of developing countries (Reiner and Sundaram 2015; Yunker 2014).

The Truman Doctrine

The Truman Doctrine was formulated in 1947 as the USA policy for delivering economic and military aid to Greece and Turkey—two countries that were threatened to come under the Soviet sphere of interest (Bostdorff 2008). Subsequently, the Truman Doctrine was informally extended to become the basis of the Cold War policy of containment (Spalding 2006; Gaddis 2005).

However, the initial focus of providing aid to Greece and Turkey was extended globally, and most notably to Asian countries, such as Vietnam and Korea (Wilde 2016). The USA pledged to provide funds, equipment, or armed forces to all nations which were endangered by and opposed to a communist takeover. Emerging from this pledge was the USA policy of containment, namely to prevent the enlargement of the Soviet sphere of influence by ensuring that countries do not align themselves politically or economically with the Soviet Bloc. Thus, it could be argued that the Truman Doctrine used economic, technical and military aid as Cold War political defence against the perceived or real expansion of the Soviet Union and communism (Gaddis 2005).

Over decades and beyond the Cold War era, the USA has become involved in all regions of the globe. Its aim remains basically the same—to maintain and expand its own economic and political sphere of interests by promoting its values and norms through development, as well as military aid. The Truman Doctrine has prevailed in one form or another and has maintained its political importance and relevance to date.

The argument follows. Firstly, the Truman Doctrine called on the USA to provide global leadership to ensure democracy, maintain peace, and advance economic prosperity, globally (Mallalieu 1958). Secondly, the Truman Doctrine acknowledges that foreign intervention includes political, economic, and military actions and that these are neither mutually exclusive nor co-dependent. This means that foreign interventions may go beyond, and may even exclude military actions, focussing entirely on economic interventions, such as financial and technical aid. It may also mean that foreign aid is withdrawn or curtailed. Today, the recognition of wide-reaching effects of economic and political interventions, enable the USA to adjust its foreign relation, including development aid policies, at bilateral and multilateral levels (Atwood et al. 2008; Burnside and Dollar 1997). Thirdly, the Truman Doctrine has over decades defined how the USA manages foreign interventions. It supposes that abdicating the responsibility of safeguarding welfare and social and political stability globally, leads to potential conflict. From this vantage point it has been recognised by most, if not all USA administrations up until now, that a global interrelation is essential (Fleck and Kilby 2010)

These three features of the Truman Doctrine have remained relevant until the rise of populism and the inauguration of Donald Trump as the President of the USA. It will be interesting to observe how the Trump administration will engage with the principles of the Truman Doctrine.

The Truman Point Four Programme

The Point Four Program was the first global USA foreign aid technical assistance program, and it was articulated by President Truman in his inaugural speech in 1949 (Committee on Foreign Affairs 1949). Arguably the Point Four Program, when compared to the Truman Doctrine and the Marshall Plan was richer and more enduring. With the Point Four Program, Truman proclaimed a new USA foreign aid policy, which was to redress the economic backwardness (cf. Gerschenkron 1962) of developing countries. The Point Four program was to assist '…the development of the economically underdeveloped areas by making available technical resources and, on a cooperative basis, fostering capital investment in them' (Committee on Foreign Affairs 1949, p. 1). Truman argued against the formerly existing system of imperialism which he perceived as a for-profit manipulation at the expense of developing countries (Macekura 2013). Truman's Point Four Program had political as well as economic aims. Not dissimilar to the Truman Doctrine the Program's political purpose was to avert the potential of unstable nations to become part of the communist camp. Concurrently, the economic aims were to create markets for USA through poverty reduction and increase production in developing countries (Aksamit 2011). The poverty reduction thesis is today as relevant and applicable within the political realm of IFIs as it was at its proclamation in 1949.

The Point Four Program was not without its critics. Some argued that foreign aid as envisaged by the Four Point Program is akin to neo-imperialism, an enticement given to the political elites in developing nations to use for improving the economic and political conditions of the population. Such improvement, so the criticism goes, is seldom successful. Others argued that the program is based on Anglo-American superiority and blindly links modernisation in aid-recipient developing countries to the Western capitalist model. Conservative political forces argued that foreign aid as articulated by Truman represents liberal suppositions about state governance and the economy, which are insupportable (Delton 2013).

The Washington Consensus Epoch as a Neoliberal Manifesto

Following the short historical-political overview and changes discussed in the first part of this chapter, the dominant Washington Consensus Doctrine is cast as a neoliberal manifesto (Marangos 2009). It is shown that the values of the Washington Consensus are couched in the free-market ideology of Friedman and Hayek. To elucidate:

> The term 'Washington Consensus', as Williamson the father of the term conceived it, in 1989, was a set of reforms for economic development that he [Williams] judged 'Washington' could agree were required in Latin America. However, the Washington Consensus has been identified as a neoliberal manifesto and calls were made for the implementation of a different set of policies, which took the form of the 'Augmented Washington Consensus' (Marangos 2009, p. 197).

The ten policy reforms identified by Williamson (1989) are: (i) fiscal policy discipline; (ii) redirecting public spending from subsidies; (iii) tax reforms; (iv) market determined interest rates; (v) competitive exchange rates; (vi) trade liberalisation; (vii) liberalisation of inward foreign investment; (viii) privatisation of state enterprises; (ix) deregulation and abolition of regulations that impede market entry or restrict competition; and (x) legal security for private property. Perhaps not all of these ten points represent neoliberalism. For example, the redirecting of public spending from subsidies could be interpreted as switching expenditure in a pro-poor way, say from indiscriminate subsidies to basic health and education.

Williamson rejected the various usages of the term 'Washington Consensus'. Originally it was a list of policies which he perceived as being widely accepted by 'Washington' institutions (i.e., the IMF and the World Bank), that were intended to be imposed from 1989 on Latin American countries. Perhaps more relevant is Williamson's second specific meaning of the Washington Consensus. He defined it as a series of economic policies imposed on developing nations by the aforesaid IFIs and the USA Treasury. Today, one may add regional aid organisations, such as the ADB, AfDB, EBRD, who follow in their footsteps.

Williamson laments that critics of the Washington Consensus accuse the IFIs of being representatives of neoliberalism. He seems to reject this criticism by arguing that there is insufficient literature to support such assertions. On this point Williamsons claim is curious, especially since embedded in the above ten points are ideologies that support macroeconomic discipline (Friedman 1962; Friedman and Schwartz 1963), market economy (Friedman 1962, 1980) and trade openness to the world economies (Munck 2005; Mises 1962; Nozick 1974; Hayek1979). Having its ideological roots in the thoughts of Friedman and Hayek it is not surprising that the Washington Consensus was labelled a 'neoliberal manifesto' and received much criticism (Stiglitz 1998a).

However, a cautionary note is here in place, namely there is much debate in the scholarly literature if Hayek and Friedman were neoliberal thinkers. If, for example, we turn to works of Blomgren (1997), Harvey (2005) and Boneau (2004) the political and economic theories of both Hayek's and Friedman's thoughts are described as neoliberal philosophy. Yet at the same time their work is attributed to theoretical foundations different from traditional neoliberal political norms. For example, Friedman's work represents consequential neoliberalism meaning that he advocates neoliberal policies such as drastic tax cuts, privatisation and deregulation. The rationale is that these measures will have positive impact on political-economic situation (cf. Friedman 1962, 1980). Not dissimilar, Hayek may be seen as a more conservative neoliberal. That is, Hayek at times articulates a functional line of reasoning in support of neoliberalism. Similar to Friedman's propositions he advocates in favour of securing social live based on individual liberties (cf. Hayek 1944, 1973).

Although, the above categorisation of Friedman's work may be seen as a form of consequential neoliberalism and Hayek's work akin to conservative neoliberalism this proposition is obviously somewhat problematic. It could be argued that other understandings of Friedman's and Hayek's thought is possible, especially if one were to view neoliberalism as a broadly delineated collection of ideas and political and economic beliefs. They have a common grounding in the assertion that the only authentic purpose of the government is to protect commercial and property rights of individual. Thus, it remains open as to which extent both, Freeman and Hayek may be seen as neoliberals.

Turning to development aid, many, if not all ten Washington Consensus points are being implemented by the IFIs and other regional and bilateral aid agencies as neoliberal 'conditionalities' for loan and grant allocation (Jakupec and Kelly 2016). From this vantage point it can be argued that the rise of neoliberal Washington Consensus in the development aid arena, expressed as conditionalities on developing economies, depicts not only an era of devaluing thinking (cf. Jakupec and Kelly 2016; Rafter and Singer 2001) but also a prescriptiveness of values and norms. Neoliberalism maintained its grip on development aid as a rejection of Keynesianism, interventionism and mono-economics. The problem however was, and still is, that neoliberalism offered little epistemological impetus and relied extensively on the unquestioned belief in the magnanimity of the free markets, supported by notions of privatisation and deregulation. This neoliberal world view effectively rejected any critical thinking in the development aid arena from a social sciences point of view, and almost completely silenced critical approaches in development studies. As it was noted in Chapter 1, the demise of the Soviet Union and the end of the Cold war was perceived as the final victory of capitalism (cf. Fukuyama 1989, 1992). Until recently, the economic thinking within the IFIs was based on the cult of economic efficiency, requiring the developing nations to adopt fiscal rectitude, privatisation, free trade, and limited government interventions into the economy.

The Failure of the Washington Consensus and the Rise of the Post-Washington Consensus

Stiglitz (1998a) introduced the term 'post-Washington Consensus' as a critique of the dominant economic Doctrine underpinning the Washington Consensus. Following the GFC the critique gained increased acceptance within the development aid arena. This led to continuing challenges of the Washington Consensus politico-economic orthodoxies, which dominated the development aid since the 1980s by development economists such as Krugman (1995a, b, 2008), Sachs (2005) and Easterly (2005) to name but a few.

The most prominent economic critics are Stiglitz (1998a, b) and Krugman (1995a, b). Both argue that following the imposition of Washington Consensus policies on developing countries economic success was not forthcoming, or at least not as forthcoming as it was claimed to be by the Washington Consensus institutions. The conditionalities for accepting structural adjustment programs and macroeconomic stabilisation reforms did not yield the economic recoveries promised by IFIs.

Stiglitz (2008, p. 41) contends:

> If there is a consensus today about what strategies are most likely to promote the development of the poorest countries in the world, it is this: There is no consensus except that the Washington Consensus did not provide the answer. Its recipes were neither necessary nor sufficient for successful growth.

However, Stiglitz (2008, p. 41) advances a partial disclaimer, namely that Washington Consensus policies, '…made sense for particular countries at particular times'. He argued that the Washington Consensus institution paid too much attention to economics at the expense of a broader context of development aid (Stiglitz 1998b, 2001). In other words, Stiglitz (1998a, b) critique focusses on the Washington Consensus institution's one-dimensional view of the mainstream development economists, who perceived development as a simple technical problem which requires simple technical solutions. These are mainly based on neoliberal notions such as free-market-oriented allocation of resources, privatisation, removal of trade barriers and increased capital stock. The problem was that Washington Consensus development economists failed to take into account the more complex and broader issues of participatory approaches and social, societal and cultural aspects of the development aid recipient countries (Stiglitz 2001; Stiglitz and Greenwald 2003). The neoliberal Washington Consensus strategies to achieve economic development and growth are in stark contrast to the successful strategies adopted by East and South-East Asian aid recipient countries, where the government took a leading economic governance role.

The major criticism of the Washington Consensus institutions from a recipient country is these institutions promote the interest of the USA hegemony by advancing its dominant neoliberal ideology. In this ideological framework, the IFIs cannot tolerate different and competing ideologies which refute the development aid ideologies they have embraced. In order to show success of neoliberal Washington Consensus policies IFIs, such as the World Bank, claim (albeit wrongly) that East and South-East developing countries, such as PR China and Vietnam, have been following a neoliberal model advocated by the Washing Consensus institutions (Hayton 2010; Sachs and Woo 2000). Nevertheless, Stiglitz (2008) states that the post-Washington Consensus has reached a consensus namely, the acknowledgment of the limits of the market fundamentalism theory, its history and a confusion of ends with objectives. He cites that liberalisation and privatisation were seen as ends in themselves (p. 48).

Not dissimilar, Krugman (1995a, b) stipulated that despite the benefits of free trade and investment flows, the Washington Consensus institutions are giving too much credence to their economic success in the developing countries. Having said that, Krugman is in favour of free-market economics. He highlights the validity and relevance of the original Ricardian free international trade theory critiquing anti-globalisation movements (Krugman 1995a; Ruffin 2002). But he differs from Ricardo arguing that the free trade is not optimal because markets are not always consistent. To put it in a context of Washington Consensus development aid, Krugman concedes that government interventionist policies may help to contribute to optimal results, but it is also noted that policies are as imperfect as markets. Thus, it could be argued that pursuing neoliberal free-market policies based on Washington Consensus and articulated as a conditionality for access to development aid may lead to undesirable social, economic and political results (Krugman 1986).

To clarify for the purpose of this discussion, it should suffice to however briefly state some of the differences between the Washington and post-Washington consensus. The latter applies a more sympathetic approach to differentiated economic developments (cf. Jomo and Fine 2006; Marangos 2008, 2009) and accepts the proposition that economic development may bring to the fore significant changes in social relations within an aid recipient country, as well as the shifts in family structure and relationships, work patterns, urbanisation, migration from rural to urban centres, realignment of social services and other aspects of the socio-cultural life. Based on these considerations, proponents of the post-Washington Consensus perceive the usual macroeconomic grounding of the Washington Consensus as deficient and possibly ambiguous as far as development aid is concerned.

In comparison, the post-Washington Consensus is less ideologically doctrinarian than the Washington Consensus. At least when it comes to development aid conditionalities concerning the neoliberal free-market canon and the extent to which access to the international free market, privatisation, decentralisation and free financial and human capital movement benefits developing countries. Krugman, in contrast to Stiglitz, argues that there is insufficient evidence to show that the removal of international trade barriers, for example, may be linked to economic growth in developing countries (Rodrik 1998).

The two main features of the post-Washington Consensus are: (i) the post-Washington Consensus is characterised by its adherence to neoliberal ideologies, especially in the form of financial and trade liberalisation (cf. Rodrik 2006; Broad 2004); and (ii) there is a greater consideration of the recipient country's socio-economic needs and ownership (Jakupec and Kelly 2016), when compared to the Washington Consensus (cf. Önis and Senses 2003; Gore 2000).

To conclude, there is limited evidence that the Washington Consensus institutions have advanced beyond their neoliberal ideology with its market fundamentalism and economic globalisation. Even with acknowledgment by IFIs to consider socio-economic impacts of development aid, economic development takes precedence over social, political and cultural constitutions of the development aid recipient country. The limited evidence concerning ideological change between Washington and post-Washington Consensus does not provide for replacement of neoliberal dogma. The changes are supplementary; namely, there is an expansion and adjustment of the Washington Consensus, leading to the post-Washington Consensus. From this vantage point, post-Washington Consensus is a variant of its predecessor still holding on to the former political, intellectual and ideological roots and the dogma of privatisation, foreign direct investment inflows, and liberalisation of imports. Stiglitz's (2008) question, 'Is there a "post-Washington Consensus" consensus?' remains.

Economic Globalisation as a Development Aid Cornerstone

The concept called 'globalisation' provokes different reactions and responses within the development aid arena. Some regard it with hostility, while others see it as the manifestation of a new world order bringing about increased economic, cultural, military, political and social homogeneity. Thus, as a term, globalisation explains a broad phenomenon and elucidates the problems associated with the new post-Cold War world order. There is a wide range of interpretation and understandings of the term by a wide range of academic disciplines, such as historians, social scientists, economists, political science, human geographers, philosophers, anthropologists and many other academic disciplines. Given the hugely diverse conceptualisation across the disciplines, only a very small and limited insight into globalisation as it relates to development aid is provided.

Arguably, globalisation is the dominant development aid theme of the past thirty years, influencing not only the economic but also the social, cultural and political structures of the developing countries. The term 'globalisation' is often used and criticised as synonymous with Washington Consensus and neoliberalism (Williamson 2002). The scholarly literature differentiates between financial globalisation (Das 2010), military globalisation (Held et al. 1999), cultural globalisation (Mc Grew 1992), ideological globalisation (Soborski 2012), political globalisation (Stehr 2009) and economic globalisation (Mann 2013; Bhagwati 2004). Although there are some overlaps between these notions of globalisation in this discussion, the emphasis is on economic globalisation. Acknowledging the danger of over-simplification, economic globalisation, for the purpose of this discussion, is defined as the means of integration of national economies into international economy, by way of free flow of goods, services, and labour through reduction of trade barriers (Stiglitz 2002; Bhagwati 2004).

The very concept of economic globalisation as far as development aid is concerned, is governed and defined by the IMF, the World Bank and other development aid institutions following the Washington and, lately, the post-Washington Consensus. Indisputably, IMF and the World Bank institutions exert immense influence and power over developing countries' economies. Conversely, both institutions are subjected to the wishes and dictates of the powerful contributor nations such as the USA. Thus, there is a direct link between the aid policies of the USA and other developed economies and Washington Consensus institutions.

Following from the analysis concerning the failure of the Washington Consensus and the aforesaid feeling of disenfranchisement of sections of society in the Western development aid-contributing countries, an important question arises: Is globalisation, within the context of development aid as we know it, coming to an end? The IFI response is that globalisation is not only an economically highly desirable but also unstoppable (Hebron and Stack 2017). Against this assertion, the populist movement asserts that governments in both the developed and developing countries need to withdraw from the policies of neoliberal globalisation and embrace nationalism and nationalist values. In between is the argument that although the impetus towards economic globalisation is slowing down, it has not been reversed. The reasons for this slow down are given as the level of high unemployment in high-income countries and the after-effects of the GFC, as much as the continuing European Monetary Crisis (Wolff 2013).

Trump has used the example of the high unemployment rate generally and specifically in the Rust Belt of the USA, arguably caused by forces of economic globalisation, as a platform for his foreign trade and development aid policies. He and other populist political leaders like Wilders and Le Pen have declared war on globalisation. Presently, due to his political power, only Trump is in the position to destabilise 'the post-war global order...' (Goroff 2017, n.p.). Following Trump's rhetoric concerning free-trade agreements, we may ask the question: Is the form of globalisation as we know it coming to an end? The World Bank suggests it is not. González (2016, n.p.) World Bank Senior Director, Trade and Competitiveness Global Practice, argues 'globalisation is the only answer'. Using the presidential election in USA and Brexit as an example, she is correctly suggesting '...that public distrust of global integration is on the rise, and that this distrust could derail new trade agreements currently in the works, and prevent future ones from being initiated' (n.p.). She continues in defence of globalisation noting that '... just because managing the effects of globalisation is difficult does not mean we should throw our hands up and quit' (n.p.). The basic argument in favour of globalisation as far as the development aid is concerned is that free and open markets benefit both the developed and developing economies (IMF 2006; Buira 2003). Failing this, globalisation as a cooperative economic structure and as a conditionality for development aid loans may turn into international economic conflicts González (2016).

The basic arguments that support the concept of neoliberal globalisation as a cornerstone of development aid conditionalities include: that recipient countries should develop and implement policies ensuring privatisation of state-owned enterprises, deregulation, liberalisation of imports and foreign direct investment inflows and interest rates, as well as legislate to minimise the role of the government intervention into the economy (Held 2008). Against this, the populist and other movements, such as various labour groups (Evans 2000), anti-corporate globalisation movements (Starr and Adams 2003) and the social justice movements (Goldman 2005) reject globalisation as something that must be feared as it promotes great disparities between the rich and the poor. This is in stark contrast to the supporters of globalisation who welcome it as the catalyst for a new world order by breaking down economic, political, social and cultural barriers.

The current reality is that working class and lower middle class are frustrated and disillusioned, and they are expressing these feelings in elections across many Western countries. In this context, globalisation takes on a new meaning. One of the problems is that proponents of globalisation have promised over past decades that each generation will be economically and socially better off than the previous one. The same argument is being propagated in developing countries through development aid conditionalities, namely that neoliberal globalisation will mitigate trans-generational poverty. However, as history has shown this is not a forgone conclusion. In many instances, the development aid brought about an economic downward trend. As Wolff (2013) notes, although globalisation has helped to reduce poverty in developing countries, it has also brought about great strain and anxiety as manufacturing has moved from industrialised countries to low-wage economies.

Current principles of globalisation are a catalyst for the existing multilateral foreign aid distribution. As part of the drive for economic progress over the past three decades, IFIs and national governments from developing and developed countries have increasingly adopted neoliberal policies. However, the picture is changing due to the rise of populism and national protectionism. Until the rise of populism, no political leader of either a major developing or industrialised developed country has negated the commitment to free trade as it is understood within a context of globalisation. By declaring war on globalisation, Trump is moving the goal posts.

Conclusion

This brief historic-political overview has shown how the USA took the leading role in providing foreign aid in the post-WWII epochs and became the world's largest development aid donor. The USA introduced and implemented the Marshall Plan to help Europe rebuild. The immediate post-WWII development aid policies were formed to a large extent by the Truman Point Four Program and the Truman Doctrine. However, with the advent of the Cold War, a new phenomenon arose. Throughout the Cold War era, USA and the Soviet Union and their allies used development aid to extend their sphere of political interest. There were times when meeting basic human needs was the main agenda, and there were times when the economic restructuring was the priority. In more recent times the question about efficiency, effectiveness, and impact of development aid has emerged. This has led to the critical appraisal of globalisation ideology as a catalyst for development success.

The neoliberal kind of globalisation ideology is being increasingly challenged by the left and more recently by populist movements across the globe. The main two arguments against neoliberal globalisation are that a national level economic policy remains crucial to economic development and that the global economy is ungovernable. This is partially reflected in the Trump rhetoric relating to his anti-globalisation agenda. By rejecting the neoliberal globalisation agenda, Trump has generated significant uncertainty about the future of development aid. Under his administration, the potential USA direction regarding development aid is not following any of the development aid policies and ideologies that emerged from the WWII. This will inevitably change the existing development aid discourse, which in the context of the potential populist changes to development aid requires, for a better understanding of the new populist agenda, a critical analysis.

References

Abbott, G.C. 1971. A Re-Examination of the 1929 Colonial Development Act. *The Economic History Review* 24 (1): 68–81.

Aksamit, D. 2011. *Modernization Theory in all but the name: Chester Bowles and the Point Four Program*. Manhattan Kansas: Kansas State University.

Atwood, J.B., M.P. McPherson, and A. Natsios. 2008. Arrested Development: Making Foreign Aid a More Effective Tool. *Foreign Affairs* 87 (6): 123–32.

Bhagwati, J. 2004. *In Defense of Globalization*. Oxford and New York: Oxford University Press.

Blomgren, A.-M. 1997. *Nyliberal politisk filosofi. En kritisk analys av Milton Friedman, Robert Nozickoch F. A. Hayek*. Nora: Bokförlaget Nya Doxa.

Boneau, D. 2004. Friedrich von Hayek, the Father of neo-liberalism. http://www.voltairenet.org/article30058.html. Accessed November 5, 2017.

Bostdorff, D.M. 2008. *Proclaiming the Truman Doctrine: The Cold War Call to Arms*. College Station: Texas A&M University Press.

Broad, R. 2004. The Washington Consensus Meets the Global Backlash. *Globalizations* 1 (2): 129–154.

Buira, A. 2003. An analysis of IMF conditionality. G24 Discussion Paper, No. 22. http://citeseerx.ist.psu.edu/viewdoc/download?doi=10.1.1.66.1578&rep=rep1&type=pdf. Accessed November 5, 2017.

Burk, K. 2001. The Marshall Plan: Filling in Some of the Blanks. *Contemporary European History* 10 (2): 267–294.

References   33

Burnside, A.C., and D. Dollar. 1997. Aid, Policies, and Growth. *World Bank Policy Research Working Paper No. 569252*. https://ssrn.com/abstract=569252. Accessed March 6, 2017.

Committee on Foreign Affairs. 1949. *Point Four Background and Program—International Technical Cooperation Act 1949*. Washington: United States House Committee on Foreign Affairs.

Cromwell, W.C. 1979. The Marshall Non-Plan, Congress and the Soviet Union. *The Western Political Quarterly* 32 (4): 422–443.

Das, D.P. 2010. *The Evolution and Unfolding of Financial Globalisation*. Robina Qld: Bond University Globalisation and Development Centre.

Delton, J.A. 2013. *Rethinking the 1950s: How Anticommunism and the Cold War made America Liberal*. Cambridge: Cambridge University Press.

Development Assistance Committee. 2006. *DAC in Dates: The History of OECD's Development Assistance Committee*. Paris: OECD Publication.

Easterly, W. 2005. National Policies and Economic Growth: A Reappraisal. In *Handbook of Economic Growth*, vol. 1, ed. P. Aghion, and S. Durlauf, 1015–1059. Amsterdam: North-Holland.

Edwards, S. 2014. Economic development and the effectiveness of foreign aid: A historical perspective. *VOX—CEPR's Policy Portal*. http://voxeu.org/article/development-and-foreign-aid-historical-perspective. Accessed February 19, 2017.

Ekbladh, D. 2010. *The Great American Mission: Modernization and the Construction of an American World Order*. Princeton: Princeton University Press.

Evans, P. 2000. Fighting Marginalization with Transnational Networks: Counter-Hegemonic Globalization. *Contemporary Sociology* 29 (1): 230–241.

Figaj, M. 2010. Who Gets Environmental Aid? The Characteristics of Global Environmental Aid Distribution. *Environmental Economics and Policy Studies* 12: 97–114.

Fleck, R.K., and C. Kilby. 2010. Changing aid regimes? U.S. foreign aid from the Cold War to the War on Terror. *Journal of Development Economics* 91 (2): 185–197.

Friedman, M. 1962. *Capitalism and Freedom*. Chicago: University of Chicago Press.

Friedman, M. 1980. *Free to Choose*. New York: Harcourt Brace Jovanovich.

Friedman, M., and A.J. Schwartz. 1963. *A Monetary History of the United States 1867–1960, Princeton*. New Jersey: Princeton University Press.

Fukuyama, F. 1989. The end of history? *The National Interest* 16: 3–18.

Fukuyama, F. 1992. *The End of History and the Last Man*. London: Penguin Group.

Gaddis, J.L. 2005. *Strategies of Containment: A Critical Appraisal of Postwar American National Security Policy*. New York: Oxford University Press.

Gerschenkron, A. 1962. *Economic backwardness in historical perspective, a book of essays*. Cambridge MA: Belknap Press.

Gillingham, J. 2003. *European Integration 1950–2003: Superstate or New Market Economy?*. Cambridge: Cambridge University Press.

Gimbel, J. 1976. *The origins of the Marshall Plan*. Stanford: Stanford University Press.

Goldman, M. 2005. *Imperial Nature: The World bank and the Struggle for Social Justice in the Age of Globalisation*. New Haven and London: Yale University Press.

González, A. 2016. Globalization Is the Only Answer. Project Syndicate (August 8, 2016). http://www.worldbank.org/en/news/opinion/2016/08/08/globalization-is-the-only-answer. Accessed April 3, 2017.

Gore, C. 2000. The Rise and Fall of the Washington Consensus as a Paradigm for Developing Countries. *World Development* 28 (5): 789–804.

Goroff, K. 2017. Why Trump Can't Bully China. Project Syndicate, (February 9, 2017). https://www.project-syndicate.org/commentary/trump-trade-war-china-by-kenneth-rogoff-2017-02?utm_source=Project+Syndicate+Newsletter&utm_campaign=d882b0888d-why_trump_cant_bully_china_by_rogoff_2_12_2016&utm_medium=email&utm_term=0_73bad5b7d8-d882b0888d-93848665. Accessed February 12, 2017.

Harvey, D. 2005. *A Brief History of Neoliberalism*. Oxford: Oxford University Press.

Hayek, F.A. 1944. *The Road to Serfdom*. London: Routledge.

Hayek, F.A. 1973. *Law, Legislation and Liberty: A new Statement of the Liberal Principles and Political Economy. Volume I: Rules and Order*. London: Routledge.

Hayek, F. A. 1979. *Law, Legislation and Liberty: A new Statement of the Liberal Principles and Political Economy. Vol. III: The Political Order of a Free People*. London: Routledge.

Hayton, B. 2010. *Vietnam Rising Dragon*. New Haven and London: Yale University Press.

Hebron, L., and J.F. Stack. 2017. *Globalisation—Debunking the Myths*, 3rd ed. New York and London: Rowman and Littlefield.

Helleiner, E. 2014. *Forgotten Foundations of Bretton Woods: International Development and the Making of the Postwar Order*. Ithaca, N.Y.: Cornell University Press.

Held, D. 2008. *Global Covenant—The Social Democratic Alternative to the Washington Consensus*. Cambridge: Polity Press.

Held, D., A. McGrew, D. Goldblatt, and J. Perraton. 1999. *Global Transformations: Politics, Economics and Culture*. Stanford: Stanford University Press.

Hogan, M.J. 1987. *The Marshall Plan—America, Britain, and the reconstruction of Western Europe, 1947–1952*. Cambridge: Cambridge University Press.

Ikenberry, G.J. 1993. The Political Origins of Bretton Woods. In *A Retrospective on the Bretton Woods System: Lessons for International Monetary Reform*, ed. M.D. Bordo, and B. Eichengreen, 155–198. Chicago: University of Chicago Press.

International Monetary Fund (IMF). 2006. Globalization: Threat or Opportunity? *SCC Data Paper*. https://www.imf.org/external/np/exr/ib/2000/041200to.htm. Accessed April 3, 2017.

Jakupec, V., and M. Kelly. 2015. The Relevance of Asian Development Bank: Existing in the Shadow of the Asian Infrastructure Investment Bank. *Journal of Regional Socio-Economic Issues* 5 (3): 31–46.

Jakupec, V., and M. Kelly. 2016. Development Aid: Regulatory Impact Assessment and Conditionality. *Impact Assessment and Project Appraisal* 34 (4): 319–329.

Jomo, K., and B. Fine (eds.). 2006. *The New Development Economics: After the Washington Consensus*. London: Zed Press.

Krugman, P.R. 1986. *Strategic Trade Policy and The New International Economics*. Cambridge, MA: MIT Press.

Krugman, P.R. 1995a. Cycles of Conventional Wisdom on Economic Development. *International Affairs (Royal Institute of International Affairs 1944-)* 71(4):717–32.

Krugman, P. 1995b. Dutch tulips and emerging markets. *Foreign Affairs* 74 (4): 28–44.

Krugman, P.R. 2008. Inequality and Redistribution. In *The Washington Consensus Reconsidered—Towards a New Global Governance*, ed. N. Serra, and J.E. Stiglitz, 31–40. Oxford: Oxford University Press.

Lebovic, J.H., and E. Voeten. 2009. The Cost of Shame: International Organizations and Foreign Aid in the Punishing of Human Rights Violators. *Journal of Peace Research* 46 (1): 79–97.

Lundestad, G. 2003. *The United States and Western Europe Since 1945: From Empire to Invasion to Transatlantic Drift*. Oxford: Oxford University Press.

Macekura, S. 2013. The Point Four Program and U.S. International Development Policy. *Political Science Quarterly* 128 (1): 127–160.

Magid, J. 2012. The Marshall Plan. *Advances in Historical Studies* 1 (1): 1–7.

Mallalieu, W.C. 1958. The Origin of the Marshall Plan: A Study in Policy Formation and National Leadership. *Political Science Quarterly* 73 (4): 481–504.

Mann, M. 2013. *The Sources of Social Power: Volume 4, Globalizations, 1945–2011*. Cambridge: Cambridge University Press.

Marangos, J. 2008. The evolution of the anti-Washington Consensus debate: from "post-Washington Consensus" to "after the Washington Consensus". *Competition and Change* 12 (3): 227–44.

Marangos, J. 2009. What happened to the Washington Consensus? The evolution of international development policy. *The Journal of Socio-Economics* 38: 197–208.

McGlinchey, S. 2009. The Marshall Plan, the Truman Doctrine, and the Division of Europe. E-International Relations. http://www.e-ir.info/2009/10/13/the-marshall-plan-the-truman-doctrine-and-the-division-of-europe/. Accessed March 1, 2017.

References 35

Mc Grew, A. 1992. A Global Society? In *Modernity and its Futures*, ed. S. Hall, D. Held, and T. McGrew, 61–116. Cambridge: Polity Press.

Mises, v.L. 1962. *The Free and Prosperous Commonwealth: An Exposition of the Ideas of Classical Liberalism*. Princeton: Van Nostrand.

Morgenthau, H. 1962. A political theory of foreign aid. *American Political Science Review* 56 (2): 301–309.

Munck, R. 2005. Neoliberalism and Politics, and the Politics of Neoliberalism. In *Neoliberalism: A Critical Reader*, ed. A. Saad-Filho, and D. Johnston, 60–69. London: Pluto Press.

Nozick, R. 1974. *Anarchy, State and Utopia*. Oxford: Blackwell.

Önis, Z., and F. Senses. 2003. *Rethinking the Emerging Post-Washington Consensus: A Critical Appraisal - Economic Research Center Working Paper in Economics 03/09*. Ankara: ERC Middle East Technical University.

Overseas Development Institute. 1964. *British Aid-5—Colonial Development a factual survey of the origins and history of British aid to developing countries*. London: ODI.

Peet, R. 2009. *Unholy Trinity: The IMF, World Bank and WTO*. London and New York: Zed Books.

Rafter, K., and H.W. Singer. 2001. *ODA after the Cold War: Less Money at Tougher Conditions*. Cheltenham: Edward Elgar Publishing Ltd.

Reiner, E.S., and J.K. Sundaram. 2015. Why we need a global Marshall Plan. *World Economic Forum*. https://www.weforum.org/agenda/2015/04/why-we-need-a-global-marshall-plan/. Accessed March 15, 2017.

Rodrik, D. 1998. Industrial development: Some stylized facts and policy directions. In *Industrial Development for the 21st Century*, ed. D. O'Connor, and M. Kjöllerström, 7–28. London and New York: Zed Books.

Rodrik, D. 2006. Goodbye Washington Consensus, hello Washington confusion? A review of World Bank's economic growth in the 1990s: learning from a decade of reform. *Journal of Economic Literature* 44: 973–987.

Ruffin, R.J. 2002. David Ricardo's discovery of comparative advantage. *History of Political Economy* 34 (4): 727–748.

Sachs, J.D., and W.T. Woo. 2000. Understanding China's Economic Performance. *Journal of Policy Reform* 4 (1): 1–50.

Sachs, J.D. 2005. *The End of Poverty: How we can make it happen in our lifetime*. London: Penguin.

Soborski, R. 2012. Globalization and ideology: a critical review of the debate. *Journal of Political Ideology* 17 (3): 323–346.

Spalding, E.E. 2006. *The First Cold Warrior: Harry Truman, Containment, and the Remaking of Liberal Internationalism*. Lexington: The University Press of Kentucky.

Starr, A., and J. Adams. 2003. Anti-globalization; The Global Fight for Local Autonomy. *New Political Science* 25 (1): 19–42.

Stehr, C. 2009. *Globalisierung und Destabilisierugstendenzen innerhalb des Internationalen Systems: Eine Indikatorenanalyse für ausgewählte Nationalstaaten*. München: Herbert Utz Verlag.

Stiglitz, J.E. 1998a. *More Instruments and Broader Goals: Moving toward the Post-Washington Consensus*. WIDER Annual Lectures, Tokyo: The United Nations University.

Stiglitz, J. E. 1998b. *Towards a New Paradigm for Development*. Raúl Prebisch Lecture. Geneva: UNCTAD.

Stiglitz, J.E. 2001. The role of International Finance Institutions in the current Global Economy. In *The Rebel Within*, ed. H.-J. Chang, 172–193. London: Wimbledon Publishing Company.

Stiglitz, J. 2002. *Globalization and its Discontent*. New York: W.W. Norton & Company Inc.

Stiglitz, J.E. 2008. Is there a Post-Washington Consensus Consensus? In *The Washington Consensus Reconsidered—Towards a New Global Governance*, ed. N. Serra, and J.E. Stiglitz, 41–56. Oxford: Oxford University Press.

Stiglitz, J.E., and B. Greenwald. 2003. *Towards a New Paradigm for Monetary Policy*. London: Cambridge University Press.

Wilde, R. 2016. The Truman Doctrine and the Cold War. About-Education: European History. http://europeanhistory.about.com/od/glossary/g/gltrumandoctrin.htm. Accessed March 1, 2017.

Williams, D. 2011. *International Development and Global Politics: History, Theory and Practice*. London: Routledge.

Williamson, J. 1989. What Washington Consensus Means by Policy Reforms. In *Latin American Readjustment: How much has happened*, ed. J. Williamson, 421–427. Washington: Institute for International Economics.

Williamson, J. 2002. *Did the Washington Consensus Fail?* Outline of Remarks at CSIS. Washington DC: Institute for International Economics (November 6, 2002).

Wolff, M. 2013. Globalisation. *Financial Times* (June 13, 2013). https://www.ft.com/content/12c74980-d1bf-11e2-9336-00144feab7de. Accessed April 3, 2017.

Wood, R. 1986. *From Marshall Plan to Debt Crisis: Foreign Aid and Development Choices in the World Economy*. Berkeley, Los Angeles and London: University of California Press.

Yunker, J.A. 2014. *Global Marshall Plan: Theory and Evidence*. London and Lanham: Lexington Books.

Chapter 3
A Critique of the Development Aid Discourse

Abstract Despite the fact that development aid has broadened from economic growth theory to include human and social capital, there is a lack of a general agreement as to its benefits. This critical review and analyses of the development aid academic and institutional discourse identifies some major shortcomings. The dominance of economics at the expense of politics, and the imposition of development aid neoliberal conditionalities act as barriers to socio-economic development in aid recipient countries. An inference is offered to recast development aid through reconciliation within critical frameworks of different sides of the political spectrum.

Keywords Development aid · Aid conditionalities · Political economy Socio-economic development · Neoliberalism · Development aid criticism

Introduction

The scholarly discourse concerning development aid is divided between claims of success and claims of failure. There is little in between. Both sympathetic and antipathetic critiques focus mainly on economic effectiveness and, to a lesser extent, on political and social progress in aid recipient countries. From an historical perspective, as discussed in the previous chapter, since the end of WWII foreign aid has been affected and formed by a range of ideological, political and economic viewpoints. With the rise of populism especially since the beginning of the 21st century, development aid is in the process of being recast in a new ideological, political and economic mould.

Since the end of WWII foreign aid changed focus from economic growth through infrastructure development to poverty alleviation and basic human needs, including health and education. These changes reflect an ideological shift conception of development aid, as well as a shift towards the most efficient way to achieve development goals and strategies. However, the motivating factor has always remained the economic imperative. Despite this attentiveness to economic

© The Author(s) 2018
V. Jakupec, *Development Aid—Populism and the End of the Neoliberal Agenda*,
SpringerBriefs in Philosophy, https://doi.org/10.1007/978-3-319-72748-6_3

priorities, there is no agreement among development aid donors, recipients, practitioners and scholars as to which ideologies and strategies may be more effective than others. This is reflected in the discourse, critiques, and disputations found in the scholarly and other relevant literature. It is not surprising that since the WWII era a consensus pertaining to development aid discourse is thus far elusive.

Contemporary ideologies, policies, approaches and standpoints concerning development aid are better represented through developments in the 21st century; specifically, the work of development economists such as Easterly (2001, 2005, 2006a, b), Sachs (2005), Moyo (2009), Mosley (1987), Mosley et al. (1991, 2004), Stiglitz (2002, 2008), Krugman (1986, 1993), Bauer (1971), and Collier (2007). The role of development aid conditionalities as barriers to socio-economic development is key to discussion, as well as the role of the political economy in the economic domination of development aid.

The Development Aid Discourse

Even the most cursory review of the development aid literature shows a deficit of common factors essential to promoting the advancement of growth, based on existing principles of neoliberal economics. This lack of a clear vision exists, despite the fact that development aid viewed from the economic growth theory has moved from notions such as capital accumulation, to investment in human capital, and to social capital (Gualerzi and Sunna 2016).

This discussion proceeds from the thesis that since the second half of the 21st century the development aid discourse is firmly embedded in development economics. While it may be advantageous to begin an historical discussion of development economics back to the 1940s, much has been published over the past 60 years and there is no need to repeat it. For continuity, some major historical discussions and arguments concerning development economics are included. These may be traced back to the works of Rosenstein-Rodan (1943) who focussed on economic development questions and Mandelbaum (1945), who addressed problems of recovery in Eastern and South-Eastern Europe. Other noteworthy scholars include Myrdal (1957) with his work on the social provisioning aspect of development, Hirschman (1958) who developed a theory of unbalanced growth, and Singer (1999) who argued for increased foreign aid to developing countries, in order to compensate for the imbalanced gain by developed nations. However, the economic viewpoint is only part of development studies. There are other academic disciplines focussing on foreign aid and development aid, such as political sciences (Wright and Winters 2010; Brown and Grävinghold 2016), sociology (Swiss 2016) and anthropology (Mosse 2005; Lewis 2005). Nevertheless, the economic discourse is the dominant narrative. In essence, the development aid discourse has developed from economic arguments in favour and against development aid, to arguments that point to the ineffectiveness and inefficiencies of development aid (Tandon 2008; Moyo 2009).

It is beyond the scope of this chapter to provide even the most cursory discussion of the works by the above-cited scholars. Instead, the focus is on the works of some selected development economists who represent the mostly divergent and opposing perspectives concerning the effectiveness of development aid.

A Critical Review of the Development Aid Discourse

The writings of Sachs and Easterly may be described as an epitome of the ongoing polarised debates concerning foreign aid. Sachs is the exemplary pro-aid proponent of foreign aid, whereas Easterly is at the other end of the spectrum representing the anti-aid argument adamantly. There is a vast amount of literature in support of both sides of the argument, but there is an absence of conclusive evidence in support of aid effectiveness (cf. Doucouliagos and Paldam 2009; Mavrotas 2009; Bourguignon and Sundberg 2007; Jakupec and Kelly 2016a).

Sachs (2005) being perhaps the most acknowledged pro-development economist advances a multitude of arguments in support of aid effectiveness (cf. Sachs 2005). A major contributor to the UN Millennium Development Goals (UNDP 2005) argues that development aid is a decisive way for developing countries and communities to escape existing and transgenerational poverty entrapment. Being in danger of oversimplification, Sachs' articulates three components in support of aid effectiveness. The first component is the articulation of a moral obligation for development aid. This obligation is based on portrayals of the extent and the acuteness of global poverty. In support, he uses authentic anecdotal evidence from people and communities living in extreme poverty and macro-level statistics (Sachs 2005). The second component is the theoretical basis focussing on 'poverty trap' and the 'financial gap'. Sachs argues that the very poor find themselves in a perpetual and transgenerational poverty trap. The crux of Sachs' argument is that the extreme poor poverty-stricken are '...too poor to save...' and are unable to '... accumulate the capital per person...' (Sachs 2005, p. 56).

Easterly (2006a, b) rejects Sachs' poverty entrapment proposition and argues that development aid implemented by IFIs is to a large extent a failure. Easterly's point of departure is the claim that foreign aid has basically failed and that this failure is mainly due to maladministration brought about by an absence of accountability by IFIs to recipient countries' governments, the society and the beneficiaries. The second reason for the failure is that IFIs are using inappropriate development models (Easterly 2003). He proposes certain institutional reforms, arguing against the top-down economic planning which militates against a market-friendly environment. He also cites bad governance and corruption in aid recipient countries and the negative influences of bureaucratic and other vested interests as catalysts for lack of effectiveness. In short, these factors, according to Easterly, fail to promote and ensure effective anti-poverty results (cf. Green 2008).

From a simplified vantage point, Sachs' arguments are conceptually close to Keynesian economic theory, and Easterly's views are close to free-market neoliberal economics. The former argues strongly in favour of the need for a recipient government's role in the implementation of foreign aid, whereas the latter argues against the necessity for foreign aid as it currently exists. Comparing the two, and taking into account the available evidence, Easterly's scepticism may be more convincing that Sachs' optimism for aid effectiveness. However, conclusive evidence supporting Sachs, Easterly or other development economists is elusive. For example, Collier (2007) agrees with Easterly, that bad governance militates against aid effectiveness and at the same time also agrees with Sachs that certain forms of development aid, administered in a certain manner, helps reduce poverty in developing countries.

The discourse of Sachs and Easterly characterises the substance of the overall discourse in development aid academic literature. The problem with their respective claims and propositions is that their arguments are, at times, constructed and presented precipitously and uncompromisingly. To explain, Sachs advances uncritically an argument in favour of foreign aid effectiveness. His propositions are couched within a framework of a linear development growth (Radelet 2006). Furthermore, it appears that Sachs is very much reluctant to acknowledge that development aid may have its failures. Easterly is not without his critics either, especially in the context of his response to Sachs' 'poverty trap' notion. In addition, Easterly has the tendency to provide limited particulars on statistical analyses, and focusses extensively on the 'poverty trap' argument claiming a negative or zero effectiveness growth. Given Sachs' and Easterly's antagonistic claims without due consideration of each other's counterarguments, it could be argued that both have abandoned scholarly debate in order to advance their biases and ideologies.

Moving beyond the Sachs-Easterly debates, the development aid discourse is evident at both the political and bureaucratic levels. Similar to the Easterly critique of foreign aid, development aid is subjected to critique for inefficiency, ineffectiveness and for being plagued by the misuse of taxpayers' money (cf. Moyo 2009; Tandon 2008). More recently, development aid has come under renewed criticism from the right-wing populist camp on the basis of lack of effectiveness and efficiency, and a tendency towards managerialism within IFIs (Gulrajani 2011; Szirmai 2015). The critique, however, is not bringing a new discourse into play although the tone and political and economic standpoints of the critics may have changed. Over the last half century, the effectiveness and efficiency of development aid have been continually questioned by academics and practitioners from different schools of thought yet development aid continues to be a major component of foreign aid and trade between the developed and the developing countries. The difficulty facing development aid is not only a failure to realise efficient, effective foreign aid that offers value for taxpayers' money. It is also the failure to link between the rationally planned politico-economic development theories and ideologies and IFIs internal bureaucratic structures and development agendas.

It can be stated that in the development aid discourse, there are two interrelated critiques dominating the development aid agenda of the IFIs. Firstly, there is the politico-economic development aid discourse and, secondly, the bureaucratic

The Development Aid Discourse 41

agenda dominating the development aid discourses. Given this interrelationship, it may be useful to review common political and bureaucratic critiques based on the right-wing and the left-wing schools of thought.

The main convergent premise is that development aid is located within a politico-economic, as well as a bureaucratic system. The second premise is that the politico-bureaucratic system governed by IFIs is responsible for foreign aid and development aid failure. Both the left-wing and the right-wing schools of thought, irrespective of the left-right dialectics, agree on the limitations of the existing planning and aid allocation procedures. The common critique extends to claims that development aid has generally failed to realise the aim to alleviate poverty and to stimulate industrialisation in developing countries: that many developing countries would have succeeded with industrialisation and modernisation (Bull and Bøås 2012) irrespective of the development aid (Matunhu 2011; Fritz and Menocal 2006). Furthermore, both the left and the right perceive the IFIs to be hegemonic global bureaucratic structures, which contribute to the creation of dependent states relying on the ideologies and conditionalities of the donor agencies. Such dependency shapes the society, its culture and political and economic structures of the recipient countries, which in turn limits the social, political and economic empowerment of the recipient nation.

The third critique from both the left and the right is that the IFIs use their political and bureaucratic structures to justify their own existence using the poverty reduction algorithm without effectively and efficiently homing in on the asymmetries which dominate international development aid policies. IFIs are aware that they can only exist as long as there is a sustainable demand for development funding linked to a demand for their expertise and technical assistance and services, and as long as poverty and underdevelopment under existing political and bureaucratic framework persist (cf. Clemens and Kremer 2016; Krueger 1998).

Setting aside the common criticism from the left and the right, there are also greater divergences. The left sees development aid as a mechanism of the right characterised by the domineering force of national and global political and economic elites, which militate against the social, political and economic emancipation of the population. The right, on the other hand, sees the elites as representing free-market interests (rather than a centralised government) that will enhance opportunities for economic growth and reduce poverty.

Most recently, as noted above, the critique came from proponents of an anti-globalisation populist, as well as pro-globalisation free-market neoliberal camps. Since the GFC, foreign aid and development aid have been subjected to intense disputes concerning policies focussing especially on the effects of development aid conditions on economic management in aid recipient countries. The point is that development aid is governed by and subjected to political expedience that member governments impose on the IFIs.

Since the 1970s, the dominant neoliberal Washington and, subsequently, the post-Washington consensus, are increasingly being subjected to criticism for promoting 'recolonization' (Pankaj 2005; Barney 2014). This leads to claims that IFIs with the allocation of development aid support the interests of the industrialised developed aid donor countries and their corporate elites (cf. Burnside and Dollar 2000; Svensson 2000; Economides et al. 2004). The politico-economic critique is directly related to the donor governments and IFIs political dogma. In short it focusses on imposing Western social, political and economic values, neoliberal ideology and conditionalities on recipient countries (Jakupec and Kelly 2016c). In doing so, the IFIs and donor governments make important and costly mistakes in the selection and funding of aid projects. For example, by focussing too extensively on stabilisation and structural adjustment programs (Easterly 2003; Gera 2016) and corresponding structural conditionalities (Dollar and Svensson 2000), rather than on the social, cultural, political and economic imperatives of the recipient countries.

Turning to the critique concerning bureaucratic structures and agendas of IFIs, the economic underpinnings become the focus. It is the economic setting that shaped aid bureaucracies and in doing so has created unproductive organisational bureaucracies in which success is measured by outputs expressed as loan or grant disbursement rather than technical assistance provided. Often the outcomes are based on low-return observable outputs, such as reports, frameworks, and administrative manuals in order to justify the allocation of loans which include development aid conditionalities. These conditionalities inflict huge economic and political demands on recipient countries.

The problem with bureaucratic implementation level is that the focus is on outcomes rather than on implementation and impacts (cf. Milligan et al. 2016). This gives rise to confusion between aid effectiveness and aid impact during the practical implementation (cf. Jakupec and Kelly 2016b). For example, in an development aid project cycle the main constituents progress from input to output to outcome. However, the development aid discourse is generally mute on the relationship between these constituents and tends to refer only to outcomes within a framework of effectiveness and efficiencies. Given these limitations, an authentic understanding of the effectiveness of development aid as an expression of outcomes is correspondingly limited. As Baker (2000) explained, 'Despite the billions of dollars spent on development assistance each year, there is still very little known about the actual impact of projects on the poor' (p. vi). However, she concedes that although '…there is a broad evidence on the benefits of economic growth, investment in human capital, and the provision of safety nets for the poor…' the overall impact on the population of a given country may not be evident. However, by stating like many others that '… impact evaluation [is] an approach that measures the outcomes' (p. vi), she falls, like many others (Berlin 2005; Killen 2011), into the trap that equates impacts (i.e. long-term positive or negative effects and efficiencies) with outcome (i.e. time limited result or change of a project or programme). This in turn limits the discourse on the effectiveness of development aid to outcomes. The second and equally important shortcoming in the development aid discourse is the focus on economic values at the exclusion of the political and the social values. These economic values of the IFIs that follow the Washington Consensus have abandoned the intractable political problems of poverty reduction allowing them to represent the economic values and bureaucratic efficiency as the dominant paradigm.

Conditionalities as Barriers to Socio-economic Development

Conditionality is a vexed notion for it may be viewed from at least two competing vantage points. On the one end of the spectrum is the IFIs' vantage point which sees '...conditionality as an instrument of mutual accountability' (Killick 2005, p. 93) and on the other end is the opinion that principally '...conditionality is controversial because it is an exercise of financial leverage, requiring governments to do things they wouldn't otherwise do, or to do things more quickly than they would choose to do' (Killick 2005, p. 93).

Historically, foreign aid conditionality has its roots in the 1944 Bretton Woods Accord. However, conditionality did not become embedded in IFIs strategies until the advent of the neoliberal Washington Consensus policies in the 1970s and 1980s. The rationale for imposing conditionality is that when a country is unable to pay for the necessary infrastructure or improvement to social services, such as education and health, it indicates that a country's economic system is ineffective and thus in need of adjustment. The aim of conditionalities is to develop an economic and political trajectory on which a nation is required to progress.

Within a context of development aid, Cabello et al. (2008) defines conditionality as a '...set of mechanism in the development policy lending that the IFIs use to impose policies such a market-opening, deregulation or privatisation, on poor countries' (p. 7). The World Bank (2005) defines conditionality as:

> ...the set of conditions that, in line with the Bank's Operational Policy (OP) 8.60, para. 13, must be satisfied for the Bank to make disbursements in a development policy operation. These conditions are (a) maintenance of an adequate macroeconomic policy framework, (b) implementation of the overall program in a manner satisfactory to the Bank, and (c) implementation of the policy and institutional actions that are deemed critical for the implementation and expected results of the supported program. Only these conditions are included in the Bank's loan agreements (p. 4).

The World Bank and other IFIs, with the exception of the IMF, perceive loan agreement conditionality as legally binding (Bull et al. 2006). This creates an insurmountable problem for the recipient countries. By imposing legally binding conditionalities, IFIs do not consider the economic, political, social and cultural factors. Conditionalities are set by the IFIs as donors under the 'one-size-fits-all' economic dogma. To illustrate, EURODAD (2006) states:

> ...impoverished countries still face an unacceptably high and rising number of conditions in order to gain access to World Bank and IMF development finance. On average poor countries face as many as 67 conditions per World Bank loan. However some countries faced a far higher number of conditions (p. 3).

These conditionalities are not necessarily acting in accordance with the recipient country's social, political and economic agenda, or the society itself. The reverse effect is possible, namely perpetuating or increasing poverty among the economically disadvantaged and poor, instead of alleviating it (EURODAD 2006).

44   3   A Critique of the Development Aid Discourse

One of the major criticisms of the imposition of 'one-size-fits-all' conditionalities is that by its own definition it is deprived of evidence-based policy. There is a lack of vertical and horizontal social-political integration into the conditionalities. Thus, it could be argued that there is a need for a broad and diversified approach to be taken in formulation of conditionalities that reflect the recipient country's given social, political, cultural and economic circumstances (Cabello et al. 2008; World Bank 2005; EURODAD 2006). There are in the relevant literature calls for IFIs to refocus loan and grant conditionalities to go beyond the one-dimensional neoliberal economic doctrine. Such refocussing demands are based on the argument that given the dominant neoliberal discourse since the 1970s and 1980s, the emerging conditionalities have focussed on profit-making, privatisation, and reduction in social program spending (Niyonkuru 2016).

It is not surprising that conditionality in development aid has attained a specific meaning. In the first instance, conditionality as understood in the foreign aid arena refers to policy reforms as opposed to fiduciary accounting conditions for the appropriation of loans or grants. Secondly, it is a tool for leveraging policy reforms through development aid loans. This means that aid recipient governments are required to implement policies that they would not necessarily choose freely for themselves. Thirdly, conditionalities have the tendency to be wide-ranging, pertaining not only to most parts of economic policies but also policies concerning aspects of regulations, political processes and governance. Finally, in theory at least, the donor governments and IFIs enforce the conditionalities with the threat of withdrawal or non-release of funds. In short, conditionality is a mechanism to leverage policy reforms at best and becomes leverage for dependency at worst (Morrissey 2005; Svensson 2003).

In practice, conditionalities, when implemented according to the Washington Consensus have shown to have far reaching, mostly negative, consequences for recipient countries. One of the reasons is that conditionality is falsely thought to be impacting only on economic and financial policy measures. In contrast, research is beginning to suggest that development aid conditionalities, depending on the sector, may have far-reaching consequences including an impact on social services, and cultural values and norms. However, research into the effects of conditionality (i.e., between the political, the economic and the social) within a context of globalisation, as well as all of the complexities of the neoliberal political economy (Collier 1997; Jakupec and Kelly 2016c) are subject to various critiques.

The realpolitik of conditionality paints another picture. For example, as Collier (2007, p. 67) claims '…[c]onditionality turned out to be a paper tiger: governments discovered they only needed to promise to reform, not do it' and Kanbur (2000) states that:

> … the evidence is that aid flows continue even when conditionality is violated… Conditionality can be introduced on paper with much pomp and circumstance, but when push comes to shove, all of the pressures, mostly from the donor side, are to look the other way when conditionality is violated (pp. 321–323).

The impact of conditionality on the success of development aid has not been established. On balance, in development aid the IFIs including bilateral aid agencies, have applied development aid conditionalities as a mechanism to affect policy reforms in development aid recipient countries (see Collier 1997). However, over the last quarter of the century, recipients have seen conditionalities as increasingly punitive rather than cooperative measures (Koch 2015). If this stands to reason, it appears that IFIs, especially the IMF and the World Bank have accomplished little by imposing, at times encyclopaedic conditionalities on recipient countries. There are two issues to consider. Firstly, there is an inherent weakness in the IFIs conditionality system; namely, the donor-imposed conditionalities are not owned by the recipient country. In other words, recipient countries see conditionalities as being mechanisms of external political, social, economic and cultural impositions of the IFI's values and not the political, social, cultural and economic structures and values of the recipient. The World Bank (2001) recognised that without recipient country ownership, it is incongruous to assume that donor-imposed conditionalities will persuade poor development countries to adopt reforms with which they disagree. Secondly, despite the IFIs' attempts to provide greater ownership of the conditionalities to the recipient countries' governments, Dreher (2009) deduces from his far-reaching empirical study, that '...there is no empirical evidence showing that conditions enhance ownership or make program success more likely' (p. 256).

This raises the question of effectiveness of conditionality. The critics of World Bank and other IFIs (cf. Koeberle 2005) refer to ineffectiveness of conditionality citing (i) failure to advance growth and reform (cf. Easterly 2001; Collier 1997); (ii) sustainability of donor organisation imposed conditionalities; (iii) intrusion on sovereignty of the borrower; (iv) conditionality content which does not take into consideration the political, economic, social and cultural characteristics and structures of the recipient country (Milanovic 2003); (v) tendency to use conditionality as a tool for micromanaging projects and programmes (Wood and Lockwood 1999).

The potential of donor-imposed development aid conditionalities to act as a form of economic, political, social and cultural dominance is a possible cause for the minimal impact on poverty reduction in developing countries (Shleifer 2009; Gulrajani 2011; Niyonkuru 2016). If the ownership is shared between the recipient country's political leaders and the donor agency, and if the country is responsible for the implementation of the development aid, the aid project or program may most likely achieve its goals. For the development aid program or project to be effective there needs to be a policy harmonisation between the donor's aims and objectives and what the recipient country perceives that it needs (Rich 2004). The call for policy harmonisation is important as the donor's aims and objectives may differ from recipient country's needs. However, policy harmonisation requires politics to be brought back into development aid.

The Political Economy—Bringing Politics Back into Development Aid Economics

Notwithstanding the calls for taking politics out of development and development economics (see Jin 2017), there are valid reasons for bringing politics back into the economics of development aid. One of such reasons is that an absence of politics has led to disappointing results, if not outright failures (Williamson 2010; Shleifer 2009). Others such as Hynes and Scott (2013, p. 17) referring to development aid evolution noted '...[m]any discussions on development aid are not sufficiently rooted in the historical development and the political realities of the measure'. Whereas Hudson and Leftwich (2014) suggest that '...a fuller and more detailed analytical framework are needed that can be systematically applied to all aspects of the politics of development...' (p. 72) and Carothers and de Gramont (2013) point out there is a need to integrate politics into development aid processes and procedures.

To recap, from an historical point of view the Truman Doctrine and the Marshall Plan had economic motives and consequences but the crises they were designed to prevent were political. The aim was to thwart the rise of fascism in Europe and to prevent the advance of the Soviet Union's sphere of influence. This political constituent of development aid was maintained until the 'End of History' theorem and the rise of the neoliberal aid agenda. Structural adjustment programs, austerity measures and a blind acceptance of market fundamentalism became the main foci of development aid. These have been identified as the cornerstones of development aid conditionalities. In short, politics was removed from development aid discourse, and neoliberal economics became the dominant and the only acceptable doctrine.

From an historical vantage point, it should be acknowledged that foreign aid and politics have had an indeterminate and difficult relationship. Since the post-WWII era, IFIs and bilateral aid agencies adhered to a view that aid should be couched in economic terms, for its aim is to advance economic growth in developing countries. Thus, polity, politics and policies in the recipient countries were forced to take a back seat to the economic doctrine of the IFIs and bilateral aid agencies. In other words, development aid was and still is being implemented on the basis of technical-instrumental, administrative and managerial imperatives (Gulrajani 2011) and social and cultural dimensions have faded into the background.

In this context, it is not surprising that within IFIs a culture emerged which maintains that by allocating aid funding based on conditionalities couched in the Washington Consensus, and administering and managing as technical assistance, will produce positive economic development results in recipient countries. Focussing on the economic agenda, IFIs remained disinterested and detached from political imperatives. Together with technical-instrumental approaches to development aid, this economic focus may be understandable because the neoliberal economics are underpinned by rational and public choice theorems. Theorems that are depicted as being 'scientific' value neutral, while political constructs are perceived to be ideological and value-laden. More importantly, neoliberal economic dogma lays claim to 'universal values' in the form of prosperity acting against the catastrophe of poverty. The neoliberal economic approach has its advantages; it is simplistic and allows development aid results to be measured in empirical terms. In contrast, the inclusion of politics in development aid is focussed on subjective values which are complex and cannot be expressed in simple quantitative terms.

Given the potential changes emerging from the rise of populism in Europe and Trump's populist view concerning foreign aid, the politics of aid reform at an institutional, as well as funding level, need to be considered. The 'bringing back politics into economics' discourse centres around one important idea: namely that aid reform at the funding level is essentially a political economy question rather than the existing and dominant idea that development aid is a neoliberal economic construct based on technical response to poverty reduction (Barder 2009).

This would mean that given the rise of populism, IFIs may, in addition to their technical-instrumental, administrative and managerial imperatives need to pursue deliberately and explicitly political goals, by introducing more politically informed methods throughout their work (Carothers and de Gramont 2013). However, to bring politics back into economics would mean an organisational culture change within and amongst IFIs and bilateral aid agencies. There will be, most likely, a range of external and internal obstacles to bring politics into economics.

Carothers and de Gramont (2013) shed some light on the situation, by suggesting that development aid practitioners and politicians have shown an increased interest in bringing politics back into economics by acting and thinking politically. Perhaps the reason for this is, as Wild and Foresti (2011) note, that foreign aid as poverty reduction is:

> ...most effective when informed by a good understanding of the political context in which they are made... [and]... least effective when political realities are neglected... These principles are increasingly accepted, but it remains difficult to apply them in practice, (p. 1).

This would mean that in order to address the needs and demands of donors and recipients there is a reciprocal need to gain an understanding of the recipient country's political system and goals, by applying a political analysis. By bringing politics back into economics the former may re-claim its place in foreign aid. The neoliberal economics that brought about the failures of the Washington Consensus with its self-regulating market ideology, is in need of overhaul. Politics which has been side-lined by economics needs to be brought back into foreign aid institutional thinking. In doing so, poverty reduction through development aid a multi-dimensional approach may be possible, which goes beyond the mostly technocratic neoliberal 'one-size-fits-all' development measures.

Although it would be tempting to provide a more detailed analysis on aspects of 'bringing politics back into development aid economics' this is beyond the scope of this discussion. Thus, it should suffice to mention one aspect of this notion at a pragmatic level. The 'bringing politics back into development aid economics' may, for example advance the existing Political Economy Analysis (PEA) of development aid beyond the currently existing technocratic 'taken for granted' approach. To explain, almost all major IFIs and bilateral aid agencies have developed PEA focussing on macro (or country) and meso (or sector) and micro (or project) levels, based on vested interests and power relations between stakeholders. The same may be applied to the power relation between development aid donors and recipients (for further discussion see for example ADB 2013; DFID 2009; GTZ 2001, 2004; SIDA 2005; UNDP 2012; USAID 2000, 2005; World Bank 2007, 2009, 2011).

Recasting Development Aid—An Inference

Problems facing the future of development aid, which is increasingly subjected to political critiques from the left and the right, can only be reconciled within critical frameworks of both sides of the political spectrum. As we have seen, the development aid discourse is couched in the left-right political terms and reconciliation of '...radical pessimism concerning foreign aid with reformers' optimistic managerial proverbs for aid effectiveness' (Gulrajani 2011, p. 216). Indeed, based on the above critical discourse of the development aid strategies and policies applied by IFIs and bilateral aid agencies, many strategies and policies have been ineffective at alleviating poverty in developing countries, especially since the introduction of the structural adjustment programs. The lack of poverty alleviation through development aid may be ascribed to various factors, many of which are meant to address poverty reduction if not alleviation.

Acknowledging that there has been some development aid success, there is much evidence that foreign aid is generally ineffective at best and, at worst, tends to '...cause more harm than good...' (Sorens 2009, p. 98). To take a populist standpoint, the argument would be against handing out foreign aid; donor countries would be able to reduce poverty in developing countries by ceasing to exalt the advantages of neoliberal globalisation and unlocking their own economies to imports from developing countries. From a populist point of view, this approach is not inconceivable. In fact, it is probable due to the rise of populism associated with the economic protectionism of donor governments that, in the end, are confronted by hostile voters demanding a foreign aid policy akin to Trumponomics.

References

ADB (Asian Development Bank). 2013. *Guidance Note: Use of Political Economy Analysis for ADB Operations*. Manila: ADB.

Baker, J.L. 2000. *Evaluating the Impact of development Projects on Poverty: A Handbook for Practitioners*. Washington: The World Bank.

Barder, O. 2009. *Beyond Planning: Markets and Networks for Better Aid*. Washington: The Center for Global Development.

Barney, T. 2014. *The Peters Projection and the Latitude and Longitude of Recolonization*. University of Richmond. http://scholarship.richmond.edu/cgi/viewcontent.cgi?article=1046&context=rhetoric-faculty-publications. Accessed April 20, 2017.

References

Bauer, P. 1971. *Dissent on Development: Studies and Debates in Development Economic*. London: Weidenfeld & Nicolson.

Berlin, A. 2005. *Assessing the Development Effectiveness of Total ODA at the Country Level*. Paris: OECD/DAC Network on Development Evaluation.

Bourguignon, F., and M. Sundberg. 2007. Aid Effectiveness: Opening the Black Box. *The American Economic Review* 97: 316–321.

Brown, S., and J. Grävinghold. 2016. Security, development and foreign aid. In *The Securitization of Foreign Aid*, ed. S. Brown, and J. Grävinghold, 1–17. New York: Palgrave Macmillan.

Bull, B., and M. Bøås. 2012. Between ruptures and continuity: Modernisation, dependency and the evolution of development theory. *Forum for Development Studies* 39 (3): 319–336.

Bull, B., A.M. Jerve, and E. Sigvaldsen. 2006. *The World Bank's and the IMF's use of Conditionality to Encourage Privatization and Liberalization: Current Issues and Practices*. Oslo: Norwegian Ministry of Foreign Affairs-Oslo Conditionality Conference.

Burnside, C., and D. Dollar. 2000. Aid, policies, and growth. *American Economic Review* 90 (4): 847–868.

Cabello, D., F. Seculova, and D. Schmidt. 2008. *World Bank Conditionalities: Poor Deal for Poor Countries*. Amsterdam: SEED Europe.

Carothers, T., and D. de Gramont. 2013. *Development Aid Confronts Politics*. Washington DC: Carnegie Endowment.

Clemens, M.A., and M. Kremer. 2016. The new role for the World Bank. *Journal of Economic Perspectives* 30 (1): 53–76.

Collier, P. 1997. The failure of conditionality. In *Perspectives on Aid and Development*, ed. C. Gwin, and J.M. Nelson, 51–77. Washington, DC: John Hopkins University Press.

Collier, P. 2007. *The Bottom Billion*. Oxford: Oxford University Press.

DFID (Department for International Development). 2009. *Political Economy Analysis: How to Note*. http://www.gsdrc.org/docs/open/PO58.pdf. Accessed November 6, 2017.

Dollar, D., and J. Svensson. 2000. What explains the success or failure of the structural adjustment programmes? *The Economic Journal* 110: 894–917.

Doucouliagos, H., and M. Paldam. 2009. The aid effectiveness literature: The sad result of 40 years of research. *Journal of Economic Surveys* 23: 433–461.

Dreher, A. (2009). IMF conditionality: theory and evidence. *Public Choice* 141 (1–2): 233–267.

Easterly, W. 2001. *The Elusive Quest for Growth: Economists' Adventures and Misadventures in the Tropics*. Cambridge, MA: MIT Press.

Easterly, W. 2003. What did structural adjustment adjust? The association of policies and growth with repeated IMF and World Bank adjustment loans. *Journal of Development Economics* 76: 1–22.

Easterly, W. 2005. National policies and economic growth: A reappraisal. In *Handbook of Economic Growth*, vol. 1, ed. P. Aghion, and S. Durlauf, 1015–1059. Amsterdam: North-Holland.

Easterly, W. 2006a. *The White Man's Burden: Why the West's Efforts to Aid the Rest Have Done So Much Ill and So Little Good*. Oxford: Oxford University Press.

Easterly, W. 2006b. Why doesn't aid work? *Cato Unbound*. http://www.cato-unbound.org/2006/04/03/william-easterly/why-doesnt-aid-work/. Accessed April 6, 2017.

Economides, G., S. Kalyvitis, and A. Philippopoulos. 2004. *Do Foreign Aid Transfers Distort Incentives and Hurt Growth? Theory and Evidence from 75 Aid-Recipient Countries*. München: CESifo.

EURODAD (European Network on Debt and Development). 2006. World Bank and IMF conditionality: a development injustice. *Eurodad Report*. http://www.eurodad.org/uploadedfiles/whats_new/reports/eurodad_world_bank_and_imf_conditionality_report.pdf. Accessed May 2, 2017.

Fritz, V., and A.R. Menocal. 2006. *(Re)building Developmental States: From Theory to Practice*. London: Overseas Development Institute.

Gera, N. 2016. Impact of structural adjustment programmes on overall social welfare in Pakistan. *South Asia Economic Journal* 8 (1): 39–64.

GTZ (Gesellschaft für Technische Zusammenarbeit). 2001. *Conflict Analysis for Planning and Management: A Practical Guideline. Draft. Sector Project Crisis Prevention, and Conflict Transformation.* Eschborn: GTZ.

GTZ (Gesellschaft für Technische Zusammenarbeit). 2004. *Governance Questionnaire: An Instrument for Analysing Political Environments Draft.* Eschborn: GTZ.

Green, D. 2008. *From Poverty to Power: How Active Citizens and Effective States Can Change the World.* Oxford: Oxfam International.

Gualerzi, D., and C. Sunna. 2016. Introduction: The rise and decline of development economics in the history of economic thought. In *Development Economics in the Twenty-First Century*, ed. C. Sunna, and D. Gualerzi, 1–14. Oxford and New York: Routledge.

Gulrajani, N. 2011. Transcending the great foreign aid debate: Managerialism, radicalism and the search for aid effectiveness. *Third World Quarterly* 32 (2): 199–216.

Hirschman, A.O. 1958. *The Strategy of Economic Development.* New Haven: Yale University Press.

Hudson, D., and A. Leftwich. 2014. *From Political Economy to Political Analysis.* DLP Research Paper, No. 25, University of Birmingham. http://www.dlprog.org/publications/from-political-economy-to-political-analysis.php. Accessed December 20, 2015.

Hynes, W., and S. Scott. 2013. *The Evolution of Official Development Assistance: Achievements, Criticisms and a Way Forward.* OECD Development Co-operation Working Papers, No. 12. Paris: OECD Publishing.

Jakupec, V., and M. Kelly. 2016a. Financialisation of official development assistance. *Journal of Economics Commerce and Management* III (2): 1–18.

Jakupec, V., and M. Kelly. 2016b. Official development assistance and impact assessment—Theoretical and practical frameworks. In *Assessing the Impact of Foreign Aid: Value for Money and Aid for Trade*, ed. V. Jakupec, and M. Kelly, 1–16. London/San Diego: Academic Press.

Jakupec, V., and M. Kelly. 2016c. Development aid: Regulatory impact assessment and conditionality. *Impact Assessment and Project Appraisal* 34 (4): 319–329.

Jakupec, V., and M. Kelly. 2016d. Regulatory impact assessment—The forgotten agenda in ODA. In *Assessing the Impact of Foreign Aid: Value for Money and Aid for Trade*, ed. V. Jakupec, and M. Kelly, 95–106. London/San Diego: Academic Press.

Jin, K. 2017. Taking the politics out of development. *Project Syndicate.* https://www.project-syndicate.org/commentary/china-one-belt-one-road-suspicions-by-keyu-jin-2017-05?utm_source=Project+Syndicate+Newsletter&utm_campaign=e62158094d-sunday_newsletter_14_5_2017&utm_medium=email&utm_term=0_73bad5b7d8-e62158094d-93848665#comments. Accessed May 16, 2017.

Kanbur, R. 2000. Aid, conditionality and depth in Africa. In *Foreign Aid and Development: Lessons Learnt and Directions for the Future*, ed. F. Tarp, 218–228. London and New York: Routledge.

Killen, B. 2011. *How Much Does Aid Effectiveness Improve Development Outcomes? Lessons from Recent Practice.* Busan: 4th High Level Forum on Aid Effectiveness. http://www.oecd.org/development/effectiveness/48458806.pdf. Accessed May 14, 2017.

Killick, T. 2005. Did conditionality streamlining succeed? In *Conditionality Revisited—Concepts, Experiences, and Lesson*, ed. S. Koeberle, H. Bedoya, P. Silarsky, and G. Verheyen, 93–95. Washington DC: The International Bank for Reconstruction and Development/The World Bank.

Koch, S. 2015. A typology of political conditionality beyond aid: Conceptual horizons based on lessons from the European Union. *World Development* 75: 97–108.

Koeberle, S. 2005. Conditionality: Under what conditions? In *Conditionality Revisited—Concepts, Experiences, and Lesson*, ed. S. Koeberle, H. Bedoya, P. Silarsky, and G. Verheyen, 57–84. Washington DC: The International Bank for Reconstruction and Development/The World Bank.

References

Krueger, A.O. 1998. Whither the World Bank and the IMF? *Journal of Economic Literature* 36 (4): 1983–2020.

Krugman, P.R. 1986. *Strategic Trade Policy and The New International Economics*. Cambridge, MA: MIT Press.

Krugman, P.R. 1993. Idea gaps and object gaps in economic development. *Journal of Monetary Economics* 32 (3): 543–573.

Lewis, D. 2005. Anthropology and development: The uneasy relationship. In *A Handbook of Economic Anthropology*, ed. J.G. Carrier, 472–486. Cheltenham: Edward Elgar.

Mandelbaum, K. 1945. *The Industrialisation of Backward Areas*. Oxford: Blackwell.

Matunhu, J. 2011. A critique of modernization and dependency theories in Africa: Critical assessment. *African Journal of History and Culture* 3 (5): 65–72.

Mavrotas, G. 2009. Development aid-theory, policies, and performance. *Review of Development Economics* 13: 373–381.

Milanovic, B. 2003. The two faces of globalization: Against globalization as we know it. *World Development* 31 (4): 667–683.

Milligan, S., S. Bertram, and A. Chilver. 2016. The rhetoric and reality of results and impact assessment in donor agencies: A practitioners perspective. In *Assessing the Impact of Foreign Aid: Value for Money and Aid for Trade*, ed. V. Jakupec, and M. Kelly, 61–78. London/San Diego: Academic Press.

Morrissey, O. 2005. Alternatives to conditionality in policy based lending. In *Conditionality Revisited: Concepts, Experiences, and Lessons*, ed. S. Koeberle, H. Bedoya, P. Silarsky, and G. Verheyen, 237–247. Washington, D.C.: The World Bank.

Mosley, P. 1987. *Overseas Aid: Its Defence and Reform*. Brighton: Wheatsheaf Books.

Mosley, P., J. Harrigan, and J. Toye. 1991. *Aid and Power. The World Bank and Policy-Lending*, vol. 1. London: Routledge.

Mosley, P., J. Hudson, and A. Verschoor. 2004. Aid, poverty and the new conditionality. *The Economic Journal* 114: 217–243.

Mosse, D. 2005. Global governance and the ethnography of international aid. In *The Aid Effect: Giving and Governing in International Development*, ed. D. Mosse, and D. Lewis, 1–36. London: Pluto Press.

Moyo, D. 2009. *Dead Aid: Why Aid is Not Working and How There is a Better Way for Africa*. New York: Farrar, Straus and Giroux.

Myrdal, G. 1957. *Economic Theory and Underdeveloped Regions*. London: Gerald Duckworth.

Niyonkuru, F. 2016. Failure of foreign aid in developing countries: A quest for alternatives. *Business and Economics Journal* 7: 231. https://doi.org/10.4172/2151-6219.1000231.

Pankaj, A.K. 2005. Revisiting foreign aid theories. *International Studies* 42 (2): 103–121.

Radelet, S. 2006. A Primer on Foreign Aid—Working Paper No. 92. Washington DC: Center for Global Development.

Rich, R. 2004. Applying conditionality to development assistance. *Agenda* 11 (4): 321–334.

Rosenstein-Rodan, P.N. 1943. Problems of industrialisation of Eastern and South–Eastern Europe. *The Economic Journal* 53 (210/211): 202–211.

Sachs, J.D. 2005. *The End of Poverty: How We Can Make It Happen in Our Lifetime*. London: Penguin.

Shleifer, A. 2009. Peter Bauer and the Failure of Foreign Aid. *Cato Journal* 29 (3): 379–390.

SIDA (Swedish International Development Cooperation Agency). 2005. *Methods of Analyzing Power: A Workshop Report*. SIDA: Division for Democratic Governance. Stockholm.

Singer, H.W. 1999. *Growth, Development and Trade: Selected Essays of Hans W. Singer*. Northampton, MA: Edward Elgar Publishing.

Sorens, J. 2009. Development and the political economy of foreign aid. *The Journal of Private Enterprise* 24 (2): 87–100.

Stiglitz, J. 2002. *Globalization and its Discontent*. New York: W.W. Norton & Company Inc.

Stiglitz, J.E. 2008. Is there a Post-Washington consensus consensus? In *The Washington Consensus Reconsidered—Towards a New Global Governance*, ed. N. Serra, and J.E. Stiglitz, 41–56. Oxford: Oxford University Press.

Svensson, J. 2000. Foreign aid and rent-seeking. *Journal of International Economics* 51: 437–461.

Svensson, J. 2003. Why conditional aid does not work and what can be done about it? *Journal of Development Economics* 70 (2): 381–402.

Swiss, L. 2016. A sociology of foreign aid and the world society. *Sociology Compass* 10: 65–73.

Szirmai, A. 2015. *Socio-Economic Development*, 2nd ed. Cambridge: Cambridge University Press.

Tandon, Y. 2008. *Ending Aid Dependency*. Oxford: Fahamu Books & Pambazuka Press.

UNDP. 2005. *Investing in Development: A Practical Plan to Achieve the Millennium Development Goals*. London: Earthscan.

UNDP (United Nations Development Programme). 2012. *Institutional and Context Analysis Guidance Note*. New York: UNDP, Bureau for Development Policy, Democratic Governance Group.

USAID (U.S. Agency for International Development). 2000. *Conducting a DG Assessment: A Framework for Strategy Development*. Washington, DC: USAID, Office of Democracy and Governance.

USAID (U.S. Agency for International Development). 2005. *Conducting a Conflict Assessment: A Framework for Strategy and Program Development*. Washington, DC: USAID Office of Conflict Management and Mitigation.

Wild, L., and M. Foresti. 2011. *Politics into Practice: A dialogue on governance strategies and action in international development*. London: Overseas Development Institute.

Williamson, C. 2010. Exploring the failure of foreign aid: The role of incentives and information. *Review of Austrian Economics* 23: 17–33.

Wood, A., and M. Lockwood. 1999. *The 'Perestroika of Aid'? New Perspectives on Conditionality*. http://www.brettonwoodsproject.org/1999/03/art-16313/. Accessed November 6, 2017.

World Bank. 2001. *Foreign Aid Can Promote Enduring Growth and Reduce Poverty When Countries 'Drive' their Own Development Strategies*. World Bank News Release No. 2001/263/S. http://web.worldbank.org. Accessed May 10, 2017.

World Bank. 2005. *Review of World Bank Conditionality*. Washington, DC: World Bank.

World Bank. 2007. *Tools for Institutional, Political and Social Analysis of Policy Reform: A Sourcebook for Development Practitioners*. Washington DC: World Bank.

World Bank. 2009. *Problem-Driven Governance and Political Economy Analysis, Good Practice Framework*. Washington DC: World Bank.

World Bank. 2011. *An Evaluation of Political-Economic Analysis in Support of the World Bank's Governance and Anticorruption Strategy*. Washington DC: World Bank Group Independent Evaluation Group.

Wright, J., and M. Winters. 2010. The politics of effective foreign aid. *Annual Review of Political Science* 13: 61–80.

Chapter 4
Trumponomics

Abstract Trump's foreign policy vision and Trumponomics is deconstructed in an attempt to find a theoretical framework. It is shown that Trump projects a vision without much ideology but arguably a vision with sufficient potential for pragmatism and *Realpolitik*. Theoretical and conceptual frameworks, including philosophical, political and economic perspectives, and Trump's mercantilist groundings are articulated. It is argued that Trumponomics contrasts with the 'transformational diplomacy' of previous USA administrations. Instead it is immersed in short-sighted 'transactional diplomacy', which will have a significant impact on the values of development aid.

Keywords Trumponomics · Populism · Mercantilism · Neoliberalism
Populism theoretical framework · Populism restated · Philosophical perspectives

Introduction

Until Donald Trump's 2016 presidential election campaign, the term Trumponomics was unknown. It emerged during the campaign as a descriptor of domestic and foreign socio-economic and politico-economic policies advocated by President Trump and, subsequently, his administration. The term Trumponomics continues to remain abstruse. This is mainly because Trump and his administration have shown little engagement with or adherence to any philosophy, theoretical frameworks, and ideology which may guide Trumponomics as a political, social or economic concept. Thus, Trumponomics means different things to different people, and it cannot be delineated as a coherent concept based on clearly defined philosophical, economic, or political positions, but it can be delineated as a multiplicity of these positions.

Lacking a coherent ideology and a philosophical concept in terms of foreign policies and foreign aid, Trumponomics has no comprehensive theoretical framework. Yet Trumponomics is real, It affects all politico-economic aspects nationally in the USA and has a geopolitical and geo-economic impact on developed and

© The Author(s) 2018

V. Jakupec, *Development Aid—Populism and the End of the Neoliberal Agenda*,
SpringerBriefs in Philosophy, https://doi.org/10.1007/978-3-319-72748-6_4

developing nations and their economies. There is also a more pragmatic issue to be considered, namely that Trumponomics as foreign aid policy appears to go against the conventions pursued by US presidents since the end of WWII. Since the Harry Truman administration, there has been a continuous consensus among 12 successive administrations that the USA must assume the mantle of world geopolitical, economic and military leadership. Notwithstanding the fact that foreign policy, and by extension foreign aid policy, varied in successive administration all administrations articulated an unambiguous message that USA's interests go beyond a narrow concept of its well-being and that the geopolitics and geo-economics are not zero-sum games. Depending how one perceives Trumponomics, be it as a form of isolationism (Wright 2016; Turek 2017; Simms and Lademan 2017) or protectionism (King 2017; Graceffo 2017), or (neo-) mercantilism (Jakupec 2017; Appelbaum 2016) or a combination of 'isms', it has the traces of USA's withdrawal from its world leadership role—a role it has pursued since WWII.

Following Trump's pre-election rhetoric and the post-electoral political reality the concern is not only that foreign policy and foreign aid consensus by successive presidents since 1945 is seemingly coming to an end, but there is no coherent foreign policy alternative being articulated by the Trump administration. The absence of a coherent and predictable foreign policy should, however, not be construed as a non-existence of policies, but as the presence of different policies which have at times nationalist, protectionist and transactional tendencies.

Based on these foreign policy tendencies, and the USA's arguable retreat from the geopolitical, economic and military global leadership, proposed budget cuts to Department of State and foreign aid may well be justified. This may be a consequence of protectionist and (neo-)mercantilist policies, pursued by the Trump administration. This brings to the fore a potential downward spiral, setting the USA in a position of diminishing returns from foreign policies and thus foreign aid. To explain, the pursuit of protectionist and (neo-)mercantilist policies combined with the budgetary cuts to the USA Department of State result in two outcomes which are not mutually exclusive. These are the reduction of 'soft power' diplomacy classically engaging the use of economic influences and the reduction of 'hard power' diplomacy, which typically involves the use of military power. The latter is somewhat contentious as the Trump administration is proposing a substantial defence budget increase. How this may be reconciled with isolationist, protectionist and (neo-)mercantilist policies, remains unclear.

The soft power notion is of particular interest because it is the basis for foreign aid. Yet, the problem is that Trump's strategies concerning foreign policy and foreign aid point to a pursuit of narrow national advantages. There is no apparent consideration for USA's geopolitical and geo-economic standing and influence through soft-power diplomacy, or the impact this may have on the developing countries, the IFIs such as IMF, World Bank and regional development banks.

From the above, it is possible to identify some main issues. Firstly, there is a need to identify a theoretical framework of Trumponomics, which would enable one to use it as a lens through which to view and understand the epistemology that underpins Trumponomics. Secondly, arises the need to articulate a conceptual framework that governs Trumponomics, including philosophical, political and economic perspectives, albeit from a range of vantage points. This would allow for a better understanding of Trumponomics as 'post-End of History' development aid politics and how it may dismantle the neoliberal manifesto that governs the Washington Consensus and the global development aid agenda.

As a cautionary note, it should be said that theoretical framework is at times wrongly referred to as a conceptual framework. Correctly these two notions are neither synonymous nor are they in scholarly terms interchangeable and it is necessary to set these two terms apart. To clarify, a theoretical framework is derived from an existing theory or existing theories, which already have been validated and accepted by the scholarly community. In contrast, a conceptual framework is a logical structure of related concepts which provide a basis for an understanding of the philosophical and practical context of the project at hand (Arts and Tatenhove 2004; Gilpin 2001).

Towards a Theoretical Framework of Trumponomics

For a better understanding, a brief delineation of what is meant by a theoretical framework follows: a theoretical framework stipulates a specific viewpoint from, or a lens through, which to analyse a topic or a phenomenon (Merriam 1997; Trent University n.d.).

The academic discourse concerning articulations of a theoretical framework of Trumponomics is wanting. This is not surprising due to the fact that Trumponomics is a new concept and has not been exposed sufficiently to academic scrutiny and analysis. Also, given that the Trump administration has to date, not been able to articulate its epistemological grounding, it is difficult to authenticate what constitutes a Trumponomics' theoretical framework. In short, a discourse concerning the subject of a theoretical framework of Trumponomics is characterised by a certain degree of complexity, for Trumponomics is not clearly situated within any specific form of populism.

Not surprisingly, populism as a field of study is a contested notion with theoretical roots in political sciences, economics, social sciences and humanities. Within each of these disciplines author viewpoints vary and populism theoretical frameworks emerge on the basis of discourse theory, social organisation theories, or ideological discourse. Unpacking the many diverse theoretical frameworks would require depth that is beyond the scope of this discussion. Thus, it should suffice to mention the variety of theoretical analyses that have been applied in the scholarly literature, such as discourse analysis, structuralism and post-structuralism, political economy, and modernisation theory, to name but a few (Canovan 2002; Hawkins 2010; Jansen 2011; Goodliffe 2012; Kaltwasser 2012).

Given the absence of a general theory of populism and thus an absence of a coherent theoretical framework in a traditional sense, the scholarly literature has explained it as a 'thin-centered' ideology (Moffitt 2016; Aslanidis 2016; Taggart 2000; Freeden 1998). As Mudde (2004) explains:

> ...a thin-centered ideology that considers society to be ultimately separated into two homogenous and antagonistic groups, 'the pure people' versus 'the corrupt elite', and which argues that politics should be an expression of the volonté générale (general will) of the people (p. 543).

Seen from this vantage point, Trumponomic populism is a thin-centred ideology, for it lacks core theoretical construct beyond prioritising the USA as a nation based on Trump's 'America First' doctrine, which is akin to economic nationalism. Beyond this, Trumponomic populism has no intrinsic principles within which to realise the fundamental commitments of 'Making America Great Again.' Such ideologies need fringe policies, such as an opposition to globalisation, or promotion of nationalism. However, in Trumponomic populism, there is no guideline that indicates the political theory that will underpin the policy methods to be taken in order to achieve the above-said doctrine. Thus, Trumponomic populism is not only chameleon-like but also a flexible ideology capable of being shaped to be appropriate for every situation at will.

If this stands to reason, then it could be argued that Trumponomic populism as any other form of populism has no conclusive theoretical framework available on the interconnection between the political, economic, social or cultural ties. Notwithstanding the numerous attempts to formulate a theoretical framework for populism generally, a theoretical framework for Trumponomic populism remains elusive. As stated above, populism has been theorised as thin-edged ideology—a strategy or a political style.

However, even from the thin-edged ideology, strategy or political style vantage points, one faces the problem that in the scholarly literature these concepts and notions are not defined consistently. This does not mean that these concepts are inappropriate as a foundation for developing a theoretical framework of populism, but they lack a generally acceptable definition. Furthermore, there is an absence of subordinate theoretical frameworks, which may provide a basis for the integration of these individual concepts and, thus, an overall multidimensional understanding of populism within a theoretical framework.

Rather than move towards a theoretical framework of populism from the vantage point of abovementioned discourse and social organisation theories, it may be more productive to progress towards a theoretical framework of Trumponomics by combining theoretical concepts of ideology, political strategy, and style (Kriesi 2012, 2013) to construct a theoretical interrelation. A theoretical framework based on the aforesaid theoretical interrelation should include three constitutive components: namely the elites, the people and the leader. Given that these constitutive components of populism are irreducibly interrelated in specific ways, it may be possible to construct a theoretical framework of Trumponomic populism in a way that provides an understanding of how these constitutive components are epistemologically interrelated. In other words, these constitutive components must be theorised as an interrelation construct, which in turn may be based on different sociological perspectives or paradigms.

Populism Restated Within a Theoretical Framework

If one were to generalise beyond Trumponomics and attempt to define it, is evident that there is no conclusive populist theoretical framework in play. The reason is that populism on the right and on the left, is couched in a myriad of theories. Arguably, a theoretical understanding of populism may emerge by hypothesising that it is either a political strategy or a political style. Such hypothesising would hardly yield a superordinate theoretical framework. The absence of superordinate or overarching theories allows for multidimensional vantage points leading to understanding the theoretical constructs of populism. If multi-dimensionality is taken as a basis for a theoretical framework, a number of theoretical constituents emerge.

Firstly, there is an explicit assumption of the existence of the homogeneous population. Secondly, there is a belief in the population's negative perception and hostility towards the elite, which are responsible for existing social, political and economic problems. Thirdly, there is the theory of re-allocation of power, whereby the people enjoy unreserved national sovereignty. However, these constituents do not support a coherent theoretical framework. Thus, the inherent problems with trying to articulate a theoretical framework of populism are at least twofold. Firstly, populism does not remain consistent over time. That is, as a political, economic and social theory, populism is characterised by continuous changes based on situational opportunity structures in a country. This especially applies to changes concerning international cooperation (Caramani 2004; Berezin 2009; Mudde 2016), including development aid, defence, and environment as evidenced by the Trump administration. Secondly, the multi-dimensionality of theoretical underpinnings does not allow for a construction of a theoretical framework based on existing social, political or economic paradigms.

This discussion aims to identify some issues that may lead to an understanding of a Trumponomic theoretical framework, rather articulation of such a framework. Given the myriad of theories, it should be seen simply as an incomplete outline of an approach which needs be filled out by others in due course. Notwithstanding limitations, it may become evident that while there is an absence of a Trumponomic theoretical framework in scholarly literature, the notions introduced here may be valuable as a background for discussion concerning the conceptual underpinnings of Trumponomics.

Towards a Conceptual Framework of Trumponomics

In the absence of a coherent theoretical framework for Trumponomics it is appropriate to turn to its conceptual underpinnings with an aim to construct a conceptual framework. This discussion will unpack concepts and their interrelationships.

Having argued in the previous chapter that there is a need to put politics into economics as far as development aid is concerned, it seems appropriate to unpack both the political and the economic underpinnings; and to see to what extent there is a conceptually coherent framework delineating Trumponomics.

There are a number of ways to unpack the main concepts underpinning Trumponomics. One may look at it from a philosophical point of view, the economics perspective and a political vantage point. To clarify, the thesis presented here is that Trumponomics is a political, as much as an economic populist concept. It is underpinned by philosophical constructs. However, from its beginnings, Trumponomics as a populist construct has displayed its chameleon-like attributes co-joined with conceptual ambiguity. Although there are emerging characteristics of Trumponomics being identified in the scholarly literature, a commonly acceptable theoretical framework is indiscernible. One of the reasons is that Trumponomics as a political economy concept is without a guiding philosophy, and yet it is a concept which is couched in numerous and at times competing philosophical orientations.

Trumponomics: Philosophical Perspectives

There are a number of alternatives to locate Trumponomics conceptually within a philosophical perspective. One is based on rational constructivism and Cartesian epistemology; the other is within the context of Heidegger's concept of Sein und Zeit.

Drawing on the works of Gherghina and Soare (2013), Moreiras (2001), and Hayek (1979), from a philosophical point of view, Trumponomics may be seen as couched in rational constructivism and Cartesian epistemology, with a focus on the notion that collectively ideas held by the population determine the social, political and economic environments. In other words, if we were to trace rational constructivism back to Descartes, it may be argued that since 'people' have created societal institutions, the 'people' must be empowered to alter these institutions as they wish (Hayek 1973, 1979; Petsoulas 2001).

Trump understands, as do most populists, that the state is an organisation created to pursue goals set by the people. His administration, being elected to fulfil the role of state leadership articulates and implements the will of the people. Since the state leadership is democratically legitimised by the people through democratic election and processes, it has a great power limited only by its standing rights, thereby elevating popular sovereignty beyond liberal democracy (Norris 2017; Norris cited in Illing 2017). This dominates Trump's thoughts on political and economic domestic and foreign policies governance.

In stark contrast, is existing neoliberalism which has its roots in Anglo-Sachsen liberalism and Kantian philosophy (Doyle 1983; Habermas 2012). This is, the state is perceived primarily as the guardian of the rules that have arisen over time through social agreement. Consequently, the state power is limited by the rules of law embedded in law. The purpose of these rules is to give the individual the necessary freedom to pursue her or his individual goals. Because of their diversity, these individual goals cannot be aggregated into social goals and, consequently, the state is not in a position to define and pursue such goals.

However, in Trumponomics the philosophical narratives simplistically expressed akin to Berlin's et al. (1968) constitutive elements of populism, namely: (i) the idealisation of the American people, perceived as being special (i.e. *America First* doctrine); (ii) customised leadership and faith in the leader's extraordinary qualities (i.e. *Make America Great Again* canon); (iii) xenophobia and racism (i.e. Executive Order *Protecting the Nation From Foreign Terrorist Entry Into the United State*s); (iv) advancing the notion of an economic, social and culturally homogeneous society (protectionist social and economic policies); (v) a concentrated use of conspiracy theories (i.e. *Fake News* phenomenon); (vi) rhetoric of anti-elitism and anti-establishment (i.e. *Draining the Swamp in Washington* rhetoric).

This brings to the fore Trumponomics, not as a philosophical perspective but akin to the aims of pragmatism. That is, each and every policy, as a thought or utterance, is evaluated on the basis of its implementation in reality and not on the basis of how it may be integrated into a system of social, political, cultural and economic principles or norms and values. At a simplistic level, Trumponomics represents the politico-economic policies pursued by Trump; there is no single theoretical framework which supports a potential definition.

The alternative is to trace Trumponomics' philosophical foundations to Heidegger (2006). In other words, a case can be made that Heidegger's thinking is remarkably pivotal and startlingly manifested in Trumponomic populism. To explain, Heidegger's place-designated perception of 'being' is inherently nation-alistic (Duff 2015; Elden 2001) and fundamental to Trump's 'America First' dogma and 'Make America Great Again' rhetoric. This nationalist focus is not only characteristic of Trump's populism but can also be found in the ideas of Wilders and Le Pen. When Trump refers to 'America First' dogma, he speaks about nati-vism as an inert and assured culture connected to a specific space, namely the USA. He suggests that their way of life, values and norms are under attack from migrants from other cultures and are undermined by multicultural entities such as the European Union.

By pronouncing the importance of 'America First' dogma, Trump appears to be very much concerned with rebuilding the political and economic nativism in the face of the dangers of globalisation. In order to achieve this, he must rebuild a form of the USA as a nation state through, for example, strengthening national borders, which would ensure the existence of identities bound to the cultural, political, economic and social values of the nation. This is in line with Heidegger's appre-hension of the downfall demise of 'spatial distinctiveness' (Harvey 1989, 2005). Heidegger expressed an uneasiness with the globalist politics and identities, which may compromise the nation state's ethnicity, culturalism and political structures espoused by the League of Nations. Trump's concern with the NATO, the UN, and other global institutions reflects this. Heidegger's argument was that global insti-tutions are failing because the people will assume the responsibility for themselves based on the elementary law of 'being' (*Dasein*) of the people (*Volk*) (Phillips 2005; Heidegger 2000).

Trumponomics: Political Perspectives

From his pre-election rhetoric to present day, Trump and his administration have not clearly articulated what path the foreign policy will finally pursue. There is an indication that Trump will, after the rather unsettled and unpredictable beginning of his presidency, move towards an increasingly stable and predictable foreign policy. As is stands, under Trump's inconsistent style there is an existent risk that USA's foreign policies in the future will become aggressive and his perspectives will annihilate the existing post-Cold War order.

Of course, Trump's political perspectives embrace both the domestic and foreign policies within parameters of populism and unilateralism. It is beyond the scope of this discussion to analyse both domestic and foreign policies, as well as populism and unilateralism, due to the complexities and their interrelation. This discussion will be limited to foreign policies.

The starting thesis is that Trump, since his candidacy and up until now, has pursued what can be designated as unilateralism. At an international relation level, arguably one of the overarching political concepts underpinning Trumponomics is unilateralism, with its nationalist tendencies. Trump's advocacy of unilateralism is based on a concept that the world political and economic order ought to be unipolar, namely that the USA is and should remain the undisputed economic, military and political superpower and should have the ability to work outside the traditional multilateral finely balanced world order. It is interesting to note that Trump's political agenda rhetoric merges populism, nativism and unilateralism neatly.

As Trump (2017) in his inaugural speech stated:

> From this moment on, it's going to be America First. Every decision on trade, on taxes, on immigration, on foreign affairs, will be made to benefit American workers and American families. We must protect our borders from the ravages of other countries making our products, stealing our companies, and destroying our jobs. We will follow two simple rules: buy American and hire American (n. p.).

Promoting the 'America First' doctrine, Trump sees multi-polarity as a dangerous political concept undermining USA supremacy. From this vantage point, the promotion of military hard power with a focus on national security and interests ensures the USA's dominant economic and military role, as opposed to foreign aid and development as the soft power. Unilateralism becomes *Realpolitik*, which is based on objectives of 'America First' and 'Making America Great Again'. Thus, for example, development aid as a moral responsibility (see Sachs 2005) is rejected, and foreign aid is only justifiable if it serves the USA national interests.

Trumponomics: Economic Perspectives

Some analysts argue that economically Trump pursues isolationist policies (Wright 2016; Turek 2017; Simms and Lademan 2017), others argue that he is following protectionist policies (King 2017; Graceffo 2017) and some are attributing (neo-) mercantilist policies (see for example Jakupec 2017; Appelbaum 2016) as a basis of Trump's economic perspective.

One of the many reasons for the diversity of perspectives is that Trump has failed to articulate his economic policies in a consistent and coherent manner. Even when he tries to convey his economic policies and strategies, they often fail to fit into a specific economic framework. Nevertheless, certain eclectic and multidimensional underpinning concepts emerge from the above stated philosophical orientations.

Setting aside the difficulties associated with the multi-dimensionality of theories underpinning Trumponomics one may look at some of these with the aim to bring it together in a coherent manner. That is, arguably one could look at Trumponomics from an economic perspective as consisting of Keynesian stimulus, 'trickle-down economics' (cf. Krugman 2016) associated with 'supply–side economics', and socialist protectionism (see Love and Lattimore 2009). Also, there are traces of three theoretical framework economic components.

Firstly, there is a macroeconomic notion consisting of an amalgam of higher domestic spending and lower taxes. The latter is perceived as an incentive for increased domestic production and consumption and is an economy couched in Reaganism and Thatcherism, arguably reflecting Adam Smith's economics. Higher domestic spending may be aligned with the Keynesian economics, especially Keynes' position advocating infrastructure spending, which was a part of Franklin Roosevelt's economic agenda in the 1930s. The second component is deregulation in the economic sphere (Bernardo and Tang 2008). At the domestic level, this applies to the deregulation of financial institutions and environmental protection, among others. Trump's third political economy conceptual framework component may be defined as an economic variety of mercantilism (see Reinert and Reinert 2011), with the aim to intensify as much as possible the economic activities within a country's own borders. This is characterised by the imposition of import tariffs, exports promotion and military build-up.

To conclude, discussion concerning theoretical and conceptual frameworks shows that both these frameworks are based on mixed metaphors from a menu of constituent parts. From this vantage point, Trumponomics within a context of theoretical and conceptual frameworks is Realpolitik—it is contestable and its effects remain uncertain as far as foreign policies and development aid are concerned. However, to view Trumponomics through a contemporary populist lens would require immersion in a mixture of the political and economic concepts of populism, protectionism, nativism, unilateralism, isolationism and mercantilism.

The Mercantilist Turn of Trumponomics

As mentioned previously there are different interpretations of Trump's foreign and domestic policies ranging from populism (Garcia 2017; Bonikowski 2016; Lozada 2016), to protectionism (O'Mahony 2017; Moyo 2017; Irwin 2017), to nativism

(Ostiguy and Roberts 2016; Goldstein 2017), to unilateralism (Galston 2016; Carr 2016), to mercantilism (Appelbaum 2016; Jakupec 2017), to isolationism (Carr 2016). These 'isms' are not mutually exclusive and Trumponomics embodies all these, with exception of isolationism. Although Nordlinger (cited in Clarke and Ricketts 2016) argues Trump is basically a populist in the USA tradition of nationalism, protectionism, nativism and isolationism, an argument for isolationism does not stand to reason.

To claim that Trumponomics is couched in isolationist ideology is at best an expectation, and at worst an oversimplified misrepresentation of Trump's emerging policies (Chance 2016; Baker 2017; Jakupec 2017). Although Trump has withdrawn from, and is threatening to withdraw from alliances and agreements in the future, he is stating his preparedness to negotiate and reconsider alliances in order to secure a better political and economic outcome for the USA. To conclude, Trump, believes that the USA should recast the rules of the international order, politically as well as economically, so that it assumes its appropriate leadership role globally under the mantra of 'Making America Great Again'. This is, by any imagination, not a hallmark of isolationism but a quest for geopolitical and geo-economic supremacy.

Returning to the question of how to define Trumponomics from a politico-economic perspective, and acknowledging that it encompasses nationalism, protectionism, and nativism, there is a compelling argument to be made that Trumponomics is firmly couched in mercantilism. Mercantilism is an economic theory and practice where the government seeks to regulate the trade and economy aiming to support domestic industries usually at the expense of other trading countries. The cautionary note here is that mercantilism does not represent a unified school of thought, but neither does Trumponomics. There are schools of thought, such as classical mercantilism, economic nationalism, the German Historical School, statism, and neo-protectionism that have a common feature—mercantilism as a vehicle for establishing and maintaining a strong state through wealth and power based on trade supremacy (Gilpin and Gilpin 1987; O'Brien and Williams 2010).

To put it into an historical context, mercantilism emerged in 16th- and 17th-century England, and is reflected in the works of economists such as Friedrich List and Alexander Hamilton. In a more recent history, Keynes (1936) work suggests that there is an argument to be made for a scientific verification of the mercantilist theory.

As Bowles (2009) explains:

Mercantilism is…a form of economic nationalism, with foreign trade used to enhance the wealth and power of one country at the expense of others. The policy implications of the mercantilist position included the limitation of imports and the promotion of exports (n.p.).

Furthermore, Bowels suggest that even after the emergence of the free-trade economic ideology '…one of the mercantilists' central policies—protectionism—continued to have its adherents (n.p.).

A similar proposition was advanced by Schmucker (2017), who notes that by invoking the 'America First' protectionist doctrine characterises Trump as:

> ...a mercantilist who only values exports, trade surpluses, and production at home. In order to abolish the U.S. trade deficit–in his view, a result of unfair competition by the U.S.'s trading partners–and to bring manufacturing back to the U.S., he is willing to introduce new tariffs and "Buy America" provisions, and to disregard the panel decisions of the WTO dispute settlement body (p.1).

To interpret Trumponomics as a form of mercantilism, one may take into consideration that mercantilism is a Realpolitik, characterised as the use of power as government procedures (Foucault 1991). To apply this to Trump's mercantilism, it could be argued that irrespective of the fact that mercantilism may be applied as the use of power based on government procedures, the Trump administration is only using it as a political approach with the benefits of the mercantile policies going to the nation. From this vantage point, it may be concluded that Trumponomics is couched in the conventional notion of mercantilism, namely as a government strategy aimed at maximising the geopolitical and geo-economic wealth and power of the USA.

The 'America First' protectionism may well lead to new political and economic alliances with the unintended result for the USA of becoming isolated rather than intentionally isolating itself. One outcome is that the 'America First' doctrine restricts imports and promotes exports—a mercantilist notion—which would render protection to the USA market and thus militate against the principles of the existing neoliberal globalisation.

Dismantling the Neoliberal Manifesto of the Washington Consensus

Trump as a populist and a mercantilist is by the very definition of both concepts anti-neoliberal, at least as far as the Washington Consensus is concerned. His foreign policies are typified by a zero-sum world view. In simplistic terms, Trump's foreign policies are based on the premise that any political or economic gain for another country is a political or economic loss for the USA. Furthermore, the zero-sum world view extends to USA traditional allies, such as Germany, the European Union and others, which Trump perceives largely as competitors rather than long-term dependable strategic partners. Thus, the best-case scenario for Trump's USA is to reject or renegotiate agreements, treaties and alliances. Trump's strategy is to convert to bilateral, rather than lateral agreement.

The Washington Consensus has conversely two main pillars. One is the adherence to free-market philosophy to be realised through opening-up of domestic markets to foreign competition, and trade policies deregulation. The other is the reduction of state interference into economic and socio-political activities. This is to be achieved through privatisation, decentralisation and deregulation, together with limiting government ability to operate fiscal deficits and amass debt. In response to criticism from the populist movement, proponents of the Washington Consensus claim that globalisation and especially the global trade has liberated millions of people from despondent poverty, and the foreign investment due to deregulation and the opening-up of markets has contributed to knowledge and technology transfer to developing economies (cf. Rodrik 2011; Saad-Filho 2010). As far as privatisation of state-owned enterprises is concerned the Washington Consensus advocates that this leads to increased provision of goods and services combined with reduced costs due to competition, and decreases a government's fiscal burden.

However, Trump has a point in rejecting the neoliberal manifesto and the ideology of the Washington Consensus. The effects of the Washington Consensus at the domestic front have had the opposite effect on parts of the USA population and economy, especially within the Rust Belt. The poverty caused by unemployment has drastically increased due to the outsourcing and migration of industries to countries which have lower wages. With this in mind, Trump challenges the intellectual substance of the Washington Consensus, even before his 'America First' doctrine is being fully comprehended and implemented. Although Trump intends to continue to pursue certain neoliberal policies embedded in the Washington Consensus at the domestic level, such as deregulation, privatisation and tax cuts for the rich, his international policies epitomise a substantial move away from the neoliberalism of globalisation and free trade of the Washington Consensus by imposing protectionist tariffs on foreign economic competitors.

Where does this lead? On the one hand, Trump's mercantilist populism and desire for restoring the USA economic global dominance is akin to economic nationalism, namely aligning neoliberalism at domestic level with protectionism against the neoliberal Washington Consensus ideology from abroad. In short, Trump wants to overturn the neoliberal Washington Consensus internationally without giving up the neoliberal agenda at home. In other words, he is pursuing a protectionist policy at international level through government policy interventions, and providing government incentives in form of, for example tax reduction to the private sector.

Concluding Thoughts

The question is: will Trump dismantle the existing neoliberal manifesto of the Washington Consensus and construct a more inclusive and equitable world economic order, or will he fail and intensify the disparity and tensions that are currently causing a rift between the economic powers and the developed and developing economies? The only certainty is that the dismantlement and replacement of the Washington Consensus by populist mercantile policies will have significant global socio-economic and socio-politic consequences in the future.

A number of issues have been canvassed here at theoretical and conceptional levels, and arguments were advanced that Trumponomics is both a populist and

Concluding Thoughts 65

mercantilist construct, there is insufficient indication that the Trump Administration will follow these constructs and develop a strategy based on the 'America First' doctrine. If the Trump Administration fails to do so, there will be no Trump doctrine beyond an utterance or a slogan from the President, and the USA will not impose its will on the world, but rather the opposite may be true.

This chapter provided a deconstruction of the foreign policy vision of Trumponomics. It is a vision without much ideology but arguably sufficient potential for pragmatism and *Realpolitik*. This deconstruction was based on an articulation of the theoretical and conceptual frameworks including philosophical, political and economic perspectives, and the mercantilist groundings. However, these perspectives and groundings may be viewed as algorithms that require long-term strategic vision and values-laden policymaking. It also requires a rejection of zero-sum worldview. As it stands, Trumponomics is immersed in short-sighted 'transactional diplomacy' (Schmelzle 2015; Durani 2016) which contrasts with the 'transformational diplomacy' (Nakamura and Epstein 2007) of the preceding administration. The former will no doubt have a significant impact on the values of soft-power diplomacy (Nye 2004, 2011) as it relates to foreign aid and by extension to development aid.

References

Appelbaum, B. 2016. On trade, Donald Trump breaks with 200 years of economic orthodoxy. *The New York Times*. https://www.nytimes.com/2016/03/11/us/politics/-trade-donald-trump-breaks-200-years-economic-orthodoxy-mercantilism.html?_r=0. Accessed July 14, 2017.

Arts, B., and J.V. Tatenhove. 2004. Policy and power: A conceptual framework between the 'old' and 'new' policy idioms. *Policy Sciences* 3 (4): 339–356.

Aslanidis, P. 2016. Is populism an ideology? A refutation and a new perspective. *Political Studies* 64 (1): 88–104.

Baker, P. 2017. The emerging of trump doctrine: Don't follow the doctrine. *Washington Post*. https://www.nytimes.com/2017/04/08/us/politics/trump-doctrine-foreign-policy.html?mtrref=nationalinterest.org&gwh=56AB17034AC2F492BA168125FE66552F&gwt=pay. Accessed July 20, 2017.

Berezin, M. 2009. *Illiberal Politics in Neoliberal Times: Culture, Security, and Populism in the New Europe*. New York: Cambridge University Press.

Berlin, I., R. Hofstaedter, and D. MacRae. 1968. To define populism. *Government and Opposition* 13 (2): 137–180. doi:https://doi.org/10.1111/j.1477-7053.1968.tb01332.x.

Bernardo, R.L., and M.-C. Tang. 2008. *The Political Economy of Reform During the Ramos Administration (1992–98)*. Working Paper No. 39. Washington, D.C.: The International Bank for Reconstruction and Development/The World Bank.

Bonikowski, B. 2016. Three lessons of contemporary populism in Europe and the United States. *The Brown Journal of World Affairs* 23 (1): 9–24.

Bowles, P. 2009. *Mercantilism*. Princeton: Princeton University Press.

Canovan, M. 2002. Taking Politics to the people: Populism as the ideology of democracy. In *Democracies and the Populist Challenge*, ed. Y. Meny, and Y. Surel, 25–44. New York: Palgrave.

Carr, B. 2016. Isolationism, trade wars … our trusted friend turns rogue. *Weekend Australian*. http://ezproxy.deakin.edu.au/login?url=https://search-proquest-com.ezproxy-f.deakin.edu.au/docview/1838233060?accountid=10445. Accessed July 18, 2016.

Caramani, D. 2004. *The Nationalization of Politics: The Formation of National Electorates and Party Systems in Western Europe*. Cambridge: Cambridge University Press.

Chance, A. 2016. Donald Trump's foreign policy and China. *China Policy Institute: Analysis*. https://cpianalysis.org/2016/11/28/donald-trumps-foreign-policy-and-china/. Accessed July 20, 2017.

Clarke, M., and A. Ricketts. 2016. Donald Trump: The Paranoid-Jacksonian history and tradition have the answers to understanding Donald. *Asia and the Pacific Policy Society*. https://www.policyforum.net/donald-trump-paranoid-jacksonian/. Accessed July 20, 2017.

Doyle, M.W. 1983. Kant, liberal legacy, and foreign affairs. *Philosophy & Public Affairs* 12 (3): 205–235.

Duff, A.S. 2015. *Heidegger and Politics: The Ontology of Radical Discontent*. Cambridge: Cambridge University Press.

Durani, L. (2016). US foreign policy: Transactional or value-based. *Modern Diplomacy*. http://moderndiplomacy.eu/index.php?option=com_k2&view=item&id=1664:us-foreign-policy-transactional-or-value-based&Itemid=138. Accessed July 2, 2017.

Elden, S. 2001. *Mapping the Present—Heidegger, Foucault and the Project of a Spatial History*. London: Continuum.

Foucault, M. 1991. Governmentality. In *The Foucault Effect: Studies in Governmentality*, ed. G. Burchell, C. Gordon, and P. Miller, 87–104. Chicago: University of Chicago Press.

Freeden, M. 1998. Is Nationalism a distinct ideology? *Political Studies* 46 (4): 748–765.

Galston, W.A. 2016. Is Trump out of step with Americans on foreign policy? *Brookings Institution Press*. http://ezproxy.deakin.edu.au/login?url=https://search-proquest-com.ezproxy-f.deakin.edu.au/docview/1797423932?accountid=10445. Accessed July 20, 2017.

Garcia, C. (2017). What we're talking about when we're talking about Trump-ian populism. *FT. Co*. http://ezproxy.deakin.edu.au/login?url=https://search-proquest-com.ezproxy-f.deakin.edu.au/docview/1870788085?accountid=10445. Accessed July 20, 2017.

Gherghina, S.M., and S. Soare. 2013. Introduction: Populism—A sophisticated concept and diverse political realities. In *A Controversial Concept and Its Diverse Forms*, ed. S.M. Gherghina, and S. Soare, 1–14. Newcastle upon Tyne: Cambridge Scholars Publishing.

Gilpin, R. 2001. *Global Political Economy: Perspectives, Problems and Policies*. New York: Harvester.

Gilpin, R., and J.M. Gilpin. 1987. *The Political Economy of International Relations*. Princeton: Princeton University Press.

Goldstein, J.A. 2017. Unfit for the constitution: Nativism and the constitution, from the founding fathers to Donald Trump. https://ssrn.com/abstract=2923343. Accessed July 20, 2017.

Goodliffe, G. 2012. *The Resurgence of the Radical Right in France*. Cambridge: Cambridge University Press.

Graceffo, A. 2017. Trump's new protectionism: Economic and strategic impact. *Foreign Policy Journal*. https://www.foreignpolicyjournal.com/2017/02/01/trumps-new-protectionism-economic-and-strategic-impact/. Accessed May 1, 2017.

Habermas, J. 2012. The crisis of the European Union in the light of a constitutionalization of international law. *The European Journal of International Law* 23 (2): 335–348.

Heidegger, M. 2000. *Reden und andere Zeugnisse eines Lebensweges 1910–1976*, vol. 16. Frankfurt/Mein: Vittorio Klostermann.

Heidegger, M. 2006. *Sein und Zeit*, 19th ed. Tübingen: Max Niemeyer Verlag.

Harvey, D. 1989. *The Condition of Post-Modernity: An Enquiry into the Origins of Cultural Change*. Cambridge: Blackwell Publishers.

Harvey, D. 2005. *A Brief History of Neoliberalism*. Oxford: Oxford University Press.

Hayek, F.A. 1973. *Law, Legislation and Liberty: Volume 1*. London: Routledge.

Hayek, F.A. 1979. *Law, Legislation and Liberty. Vol. 3*. Chicago: The University of Chicago Press.

Hawkins, K.A. 2010. *Venezuela's Chavismo and Populism in Comparative Perspective*. Cambridge: Cambridge University Press.

References

Illing, S. 2017. Why Trump's populist appeal is about culture, not the economy. *Vox*. https://www.vox.com/conversations/2017/3/27/15037232/trump-populist-appeal-culture-economy. Accessed July 24, 2017.

Irwin, D.A. 2017. The false promise of protectionism: Why Trump's trade policy could backfire. *Foreign Affairs* 96 (3): 45–56.

Jakupec, V. 2017. Trumponomics: From foreign trade to foreign aid. *Leibniz Online* 25: 1–12.

Jansen, R.S. 2011. Populist mobilization: A new theoretical approach to populism. *Sociological Theory* 29 (2): 75–96.

Kaltwasser, C.R. 2012. The ambivalence of populism: Threat and corrective for democracy. *Democratization* 9 (2): 184–208.

Keynes, J.M. 1936. *The General Theory of Employment, Interest and Money*. London: Macmillan (2007 reprint).

King, S.D. 2017. *Grave New World: The End of Globalization, the Return of History*. New Haven: Yale University Press.

Kriesi, H. 2012. *Populism as an Ideology*. Zurich: University of Zurich.

Kriesi, H. 2013. *Conceptualizing the Populist Challenge*. Bologna: Johns Hopkins University.

Krugman, P. 2016. Don't think there's such a thing as Trumponomics. *Bloomberg Politics*. http://www.bloomberg.com/politics/videos/2016-11-03/krugman-don-t-think-there-s-such-a-thing-as-trumponomics. Accessed December 1, 2016.

Love, P., and R. Lattimore. 2009. *Protectionism? Tariffs and Other Barriers to Trade, in International Trade: Free, Fair and Open?*. Paris: OECD Publishing.

Lozada, C. 2016. Donald Trump's appeal is not just about 'anger' and 'resentment'. *The Washington Post*. http://ezproxy.deakin.edu.au/login?url=https://search-proquest-com.ezproxy-f.deakin.edu.au/docview/1832993304?accountid=10445. Accessed July 21, 2017.

Merriam, S. 1997. *Qualitative Research and Case Study Applications in Education*. San Francisco, CA: Jossey-Bass.

Moffitt, B. 2016. *The Global Rise of Populism: Performance, Political Style and Representation*. Stanford: Stanford University Press.

Moreiras, A. 2001. *The Exhaustion of Difference: The Politics of Latin American Cultural Studies*. Durham and London: Duke University Press.

Moyo, D. 2017. US protectionism and deglobalisation spell inflation. *FT.Com*. http://ezproxy.deakin.edu.au/login?url=https://search-proquest-com.ezproxy-f.deakin.edu.au/docview/1875256357?accountid=10445. Accessed July 18, 2017.

Mudde, C. 2004. The Populist Zeitgeist. *Government and Opposition* 39 (4): 542–563.

Mudde, C. 2016. *On Extremism and Democracy in Europe*. London: Routledge.

Nakamura, K.H., and S.B. Epstein. 2007. *Diplomacy for the 21st Century: Transformational Diplomacy*. Washington DC: Congressional Research Service.

Norris, P. 2017. Is Western democracy backsliding? Diagnosing the risks. *The Journal of Democracy*. https://ssrn.com/abstract=2933655. Accessed August 14, 2017.

Nye, J. 2004. *Soft Power: The Means to Success in World Politics*. New York: Public Affairs.

Nye, J. 2011. *The Future of Power*. New York: Public Affairs.

O'Brien, R., and M. Williams. 2010. *Global Political Economy: Evolution and Dynamics*, 3rd ed. Houndsmills: Palgrave Macmillan.

O'Mahony, P. 2017. Is Trump a threat to the markets? *Irish Times*. http://ezproxy.deakin.edu.au/login?url=https://search-proquest-com.ezproxy-f.deakin.edu.au/docview/1860915132?accountid=10445. Accessed July 21, 2017.

Ostiguy, P., and K.M. Roberts. 2016. Putting trump in comparative perspective: Populism and the politicization of the sociocultural low. *The Brown Journal of World Affairs* 23 (1): 25–50.

Petsoulas, C. 2001. *Hayek's Liberalism and Its Origins: His Idea of Spontaneous Order and the Scottish Enlightenment*. Oxon and New York: Routledge.

Phillips, J. 2005. *Heidegger's Volk—Between National Socialism and poetry*. Stanford: Stanford University Press.

Reinert, E.S., and S.A. Reinert. 2011. Mercantilism and economic development: Schumpeterian dynamics, institution building, and international benchmarking. *OIKOS* 10 (1): 8–37.

Rodrik, D. 2011. *The Globalisation Paradox: Democracy and the future of the World Economy.* New York and London: W. W. Norton and Co.

Saad-Filho, A. 2010. *Growth, Poverty and Inequality: From Washington Consensus to Inclusive Growth.* DESA Working Paper No. 100. http://www.un.org/esa/desa/papers/2010/wp100_ 2010.pdf. Accessed November 5, 2017.

Sachs, J.D. 2005. *The End of Poverty: How we can make it happen in our lifetime.* London: Penguin.

Schmelzle, C. 2015. *Politische Legitimität und zerfallene Staatlickkeit.* Frankfurt a/M and New York: Campus Verlag.

Schmucker, C. 2017. Dark clouds over free trade in G20. *Gateway House.* http://www. gatewayhouse.in/g20/. Accessed July 2, 2017.

Simms, B., and C. Lademan. 2017. *Donald Trump: The Making of a World View.* London: Endeavour Press.

Taggart, P. 2000. *Populism.* Buckingham: Open University Press.

Trent University (n.d.). Theoretical frameworks. *Online History Workbook.* Durham Trent University. https://www.trentu.ca/history/workbook/theoreticalframeworks.php. Accessed July 15, 2017.

Trump, D. 2017. The inaugural address. The White House, Speeches. https://www.whitehouse. gov/inaugural-address. Accessed May 3, 2017.

Turek, J. 2017. *Globalisierung im Zwiespalt: Das postglobale Misere und Wege, sie zu bewältigen.* Bielefeld: Transcript Verlag.

Wright, T. 2016. The 2016 Presidential Campaign and the crisis of US foreign policy. *The Lowy Institute for International Policy.* https://www.lowyinstitute.org/publications/2016-presidential-campaign-and-crisis-us-foreign-policy. Accesses July 6, 2017.

Chapter 5
The Potential Impact of Trumponomics on Development Aid

Abstract The impact of the Trump administration's potential withdrawal from the values of globalisation that have underpinned the vast majority of foreign aid agencies since WWII is discussed. Two megatrends are offered for discussion, one is the transition from globalisation to de-globalisation the other one is the transition from neoliberal 'Aid-for-Trade' to mercantilist 'Trade-not-Aid'. Subsequent scenarios are offered, specifically how the USA's retreat from soft power diplomacy to harder military power will affect the social and political principles maintained since WWII. In conclusion, the discussion turns to the impact of USA's potential retreat as a global development aid leader and afford China dominance within a context of Beijing Consensus as a global player in development aid and the decline of neoliberal ideology as it relates to development aid.

Keywords Trumponomics · Beijing consensus · De-globalisation
Aid-not-trade · Aid-for-trade · Aid diplomacy

Introduction

With an administration style unlike any other president in the post-WWII era, and consistent rhetoric departing from conventional USA foreign policy, Trump has disrupted the global politics and security in an unequalled manner. Trump's foreign policy rhetoric is targeting the established world order generally and, in many instances, the foreign policies of his predecessor. The importance of this phenomenon for this discussion, is that since the advent of the Truman Doctrine, foreign aid in, its various forms, has been part of USA foreign policy and has followed broadly the principles set by the Truman Doctrine.

However, Trump's rhetoric on foreign policy is calling for a reversal of the long-established USA principles and values. His main criticism of existing foreign policies and development aid echo the sentiments of a large section of the USA voters. Trump's criticism of USA foreign policy, which has existed for the past seventy years, is basically as follows: USA's internationalist cosmopolitan foreign policy has advantaged the elite at the expense of other sections of the society. This

© The Author(s) 2018
V. Jakupec, *Development Aid—Populism and the End of the Neoliberal Agenda*,
SpringerBriefs in Philosophy, https://doi.org/10.1007/978-3-319-72748-6_5

is disadvantaging the USA economically and socially. Due to neoliberal globalisation, other countries are taking advantage of the USA. Notwithstanding this criticism, Trump has not articulated a carefully thought through alternative, neither have many of the populists in other countries. Thus, Trump's foreign policy and development aid agenda are characterised by unpredictability and uncertainty.

Given this lack of future direction concerning foreign policies and development aid, there is the question of impact: namely, what impact, if any, would the reversal of the USA development aid policy have globally? In order to understand the potential impact, a broad-brush summary of USA's contribution to and control over development aid will be helpful. Within the World Bank, the USA holds 16.3% of total voting power compared to Japan (7.03%), followed by PR China (4.54%), Germany (4.12%) and UK (3.86%) (World Bank 2017). Within the ADB, the USA holds 12.78% of total voting power equal with Japan (12.78%), followed by PR China (5.45%), India (5.36%), Australia (4.93%) and Republic of Korea (4.33%) (ADB 2017). On the board of the IMF, the USA holds 16.52% of total voting power, followed by Japan (6.15%), PR China (6.09%), Germany (5.32%), and UK (4.03%) (IMF 2017). It is evident that on basis of its voting power at World Bank, ADB and IMF the USA can influence the policies of these organisations, which in turn may impact on grant and loan conditions and allocations.

Given the USA's commanding influence on the politics and policies of major IFIs and its populist agenda, it is difficult to imagine that the Trump administration, like populists on the left or the right, will be influenced by the existing discourse and the underpinning arguments regarding development aid. They will not be swayed by Sachs' (2005a) moral arguments or the theory concerning the need to overcome the 'poverty trap' (Sachs and McArthur 2005) and 'financial gap' (Ranaweera 2003) even if this may benefit the economy of the donor country in the long run. However, they may accept Easterly's (2008) proposition that the 'top down' approach does not work due to the lack of accountability vis-a-vis the beneficiaries and the tax payers who contribute to the foreign aid funding. There are, as discussed in preceding chapters, other populist notions that militate against the existing views on geopolitical advantages of development aid. The previously identified characteristics of Trumponomic populism, such as nativism, protectionism, and mercantilism do not support the existing neoliberal form of development aid.

Notwithstanding the lack of a cohesive foreign policy, it would be foolish to dismiss it as non-existent. Trump and his administration have developed some strong indicators for the future direction of foreign policy. During the election campaign, Trump promised to revoke existing foreign and development aid policies. He has fulfilled the promise of withdrawing USA contributions to the UN Population Fund and has proposed funding cuts for other UN programs. As foreshadowed he has abandoned the TPPA, is withdrawing from the USA from UNESCO and has walk out on the Paris Accord on global warming. Although, the latter is not set in stone and may be subject to Trump administration review of the terms on which the USA could be engaged under the existing agreement. Thus, it could be argued that the Trump administration is pursuing critical and earnest

Introduction   71

foreign and development aid policies, focussing on policies and issues concerning globalisation and trade, diplomacy and international relations. Yet despite these developments, the Trump administration has not been especially forthcoming on details or strategies concerning development aid policies, leaving many unknowns.

However, as it was noted in the preceding chapters, there are some consistent themes that are recurrent under the 'America First' doctrine. These are (i) refocussing the globalisation agenda; (ii) greater emphases on aid as a vehicle for improving USA trade agenda; (iii) shift towards 'hard power' and a retreat from 'soft power' diplomacy; (iv) Trumponomics and its impact on the future of development aid. However arbitrary, these themes have been categorised: the first two as megatrend, and the second two as scenarios.

To clarify, megatrends delineate our knowledge and understanding of the plausible future. As such, megatrends define the current and future *Weltanschauung* and the interface between them. In this context, the concept of megatrends refers to overarching tendencies in social, political and economic environments, which may affect development aid in a context of donor and recipient countries. The scenarios provide an outline of potential actions that the Trump administration will implement.

Megatrend: Transition from Globalisation to De-globalisation

A major cornerstone of populism on the right and on the left, albeit for different reasons, is anti-globalisation. This affects all aspects of economic policies including development aid. As populist movements are increasingly gaining political power and influence, the epoch of neoliberal globalisation, which arose in the late 1980s and early 1990s may be diminishing. There are signs that Western democracies are entering the epoch of de-globalisation.

To put de-globalisation into a historical context and a better understanding, it may be advantageous to note from the beginning that deglobalisation is not a new phenomenon. It can be traced back some 14 Centuries (see Therborn 2000) including the more recent history of deglobalisation during the 1913 to 1950 epoche. Although it would be tempting to analyse the history of deglobalisation from its early beginnings, namely following the 'first wave' of globalisation from 300 to 600 A.D. (see Therborn 2000), the discussion concerning historic complexity of deglobalisation going back to the end of the Roman Empire and the demise of the Hun Dynasty in China is beyond the scope of this discussion. Thus, we will limit our deliberation to the concept of deglobalisation as it is emerging within a contemporary context. To clarify, during the afore said 1913–1950 era, the Western economy was characterised by restricted economic growth and imbalanced trade results combined with political tensions and a massive burden of war debt. This brought about an upsurge of nationalist, protectionist and populist political movements (Swarup 2016). This is not dissimilar to the contemporary conditions of national debt and budget deficits, slowing economic growth and trade imbalances at least since the Global Financial Crises in 2008.

Returning to the contemporary context the term de-globalisation was coined by Bello (2002) describing the process of shrinking interdependence and integration between countries leading to decreases in trade. This decrease is usually brought about by tariffs and other protectionist actions. Furthermore, de-globalisation has the tendency to diminish social and cultural links between countries. In short, de-globalisation is a political, economic, social and cultural construct. As far as development aid is concerned de-globalisation could have far reaching consequences.

To take a step back, it is important to note that the values of globalisation have been used by IFIs and bilateral foreign aid agencies, such as the United States Agency for International Development (USAID) and Millennium Challenge Corporation (MCC), to promote neoliberal models of economic development. This replaced the 1970s' direct government-to-government development aid approach. The consequence was that IFIs and other aid agencies imposed neoliberal globalisation conditionalities on development aid recipient countries. The USA supported these neoliberal globalisation policies using its voting power in the World Bank, the IMF and the ADB. This has opened up the USA led current development aid policies to criticism by populist movements generally, and the Trump administration especially. Trump and populists in other Western countries are advocating and pursuing different paths to development aid. The populist, such as Trump, follows a development aid policy, which advances their own national economic and social self-interests. But in order to achieve this, donor nations need to disengage from the politics and economics of neoliberal globalisation. Today, from a populist vantage point globalisation is increasingly being perceived as a threat and thus subjected to deepening criticism especially in the USA, UK, and more recently in France (Alderman 2017) and other developed nations. Given the growing public opposition to globalisation, politicians are increasingly becoming disinclined to maintain or enhance the globalisation guidelines advocated by IMF (Gun et al. 2017), as well as the World Bank and the World Trade Organization (WTO).

There are at least two questions one may pose. Firstly, does the rise of populism indicate a demise or reversal of the neoliberal economic globalisation in the development aid arena? Although it may be argued that the jury is still out on this, there are indicators that there is much hostility towards neoliberal globalisation in Western democracies and a shift towards a populist 'new world' economic order and de-globalisation seems inevitable (Goodhart 2017).

Secondly, following from King's (2017) work, the question arises: can the neoliberal economic globalisation last, irrespective of the populist opposition? The answer depends on the viewpoint and the Zeitgeist. Until quite recently, the answer in Western democracies and international organisations, such as the World Bank, IMF, WTO, OECD and many others, would have been that globalisation is irreversible and its endurance inevitable. However, King (2017) suggests that if the USA withdraws from the general support for neoliberal economic globalisation, the advances achieved over the last 50 years are at risk. The argument relating to economic progress on the basis of development aid is inconclusive (see Easterly 2006a, b; and for a contrary view see Sachs 2005a, b).

If one accepts the proposition that the neoliberal globalisation ideology which steered the development aid policies since the 1980s, is neither irreversible nor enduring, then de-globalisation is likely to be an emerging megatrend. However, a cautionary note: de-globalisation does not advocate a retreat from global economy per se but engenders a process of reforming the existing world economic system with the aim to strengthen native national economies in response to international and global economic forces (Bello 2002, 2013). With this aim, de-globalisation questions the logic of free-market economic rationalism and its global economic integration process. Thus, proponents of de-globalisation argue for the development of trade integration procedures which are focussed on promoting the interests of people and nations.

As populism gains strength, and assuming Trumponomics will gain traction in the USA and by default within the IFIs, development aid policies will move closer towards accepting de-globalisation as a new credo. In this context, the de-globalisation of development aid should be understood as a mechanism for international relations between nation states. It does not mean a renaissance of nationalism, but a global confluence in which nation states are pursuing development aid from a mercantilist vantage point.

To conclude, de-globalisation will enable the USA under the Trump administration to shift from development aid decision-making by IFIs on the basis of treaties and organisational memberships of donor countries, to the USA national sovereignty arena. Thus, when a populist leader such as Trump advocates that globalisation is replaced by 'Americanism' the discourse is shifting from global to the national economy (Bouman 2017).

Megatrend: From Neoliberal Aid-for-Trade to Mercantilist Trade-not-Aid

Based on the 'America First' doctrine, and 'Make America Great Again' notion, trade has taken on a pivotal position in Trump's domestic and foreign policies. This is different to the positions taken by previous administrations, that focussed on social issues (like the Obama administration), instead of trade barriers and tariffs.

Populists on the right perceive development aid as an economic activity. In line with the Republican Party view, Trump has decried the level of USA's participation and support for existing development aid policies, including the Aid-for-Trade (AfT) principles. Trump's main contention is the 'return on investment', namely the lack of benefits for the USA. To clarify, the purpose of AfT is to assist developing economies to benefit from the global trading system and utilise trade as a mechanism for economic growth and development. Thus, AfT is intertwined with the concept of globalisation.

Yet trade was prominent in both the Trump's and Sanders' election campaigns and captured the imagination of the electorate on both the right and the left. Issues concerning trade appealed to voters ranging from those who lost their jobs in manufacturing industries and small manufacturing businesses. Trade as an electoral issue became such an effective strategy that it compelled Hillary Clinton to retreat from her initial support for TPPA and the Transatlantic Trade and Investment Partnership (TTIP).

The Trump administration's continuing focus on trade demonstrates the potential direction of foreign policy and development aid. The policy emphasises the need to review 'deals' made by previous administrations in support of unconstrained neoliberal globalisation, which is held responsible for generating growing inequity at the national level. It prompted Trump to review the consequences of multilateral trade alliances, leading to, for example, USA withdrawal from the UNESCO and TPPA, and TTIP and the announcement to renegotiate NAFTA and KOTUS. With these actions, Trump has moved against existing international conventions, namely against anything that appears to be even vaguely global-neoliberal free-trade oriented.

However, the problem with rejecting globalised neoliberal trade principles and agreements is where to draw the line between free-trade and isolationism? Focussing on the latter will cause unforeseen consequences for the domestic export market and international uneasiness among the development aid institutions and aid recipient developing countries. In order to realise his trade policies based on the 'Making America Great Again' narrative and to implement the 'America First' doctrine, the Trump administration would have to scale back the existing neoliberal Aid-for-Trade (AfT) agenda and, in order to avoid an isolationist economy, move towards a mercantile Trade-not-Aid (TnA) position.

To clarify, AfT is difficult to define, for it means different things to different people (see WTO 2015a, b). IMF (cited in Dorsey 2007, p. 1) defines AfT as "…aid that finances trade-related technical assistance, trade-related infrastructure, and aid to developing productive capacity". AfT was introduced as a concept by the Ministerial meeting of the World Trade Organisation (WTO) in Hong Kong in 2005. It is intended to assist developing economies to participate in global trade. The term has since become a 'catch-all' phrase in the development aid vocabulary of the World Bank, IMF, WTO, OECD, and most if not all regional development aid institutions (Negin 2014).

AnT is an economic initiative based on the belief that the most successful strategy to advance economic progress in developing countries, is to stimulate free trade rather than provide direct development aid (Gallagher 2011). TnA is based on the proposition that if developing countries were capable to trade freely with developed economies, they would have a dependable income and thus would not be too dependent on development aid to pursue development projects. International trade between donor and recipient development aid countries, so the argument goes, would raise income and improve living standards, because the developing countries would have the opportunity to export their products, goods and services. From this vantage point, the Trade-not-Aid (TnA) concept accentuates the importance of establishing export industries aimed at increasing development; it is akin to the poverty reduction theory (see Goldin and Reinert 2007). Both, TnA and the poverty reduction theory highlight the importance of establishing export sectors with the aim to increase economic development.

Both AfT and TnA concepts fall within the neoliberal globalisation agenda. Both are seen as economic, rather than political or social development activities. In short, the argument in favour of TnA is that 'aid' will not promote development—only trade can achieve that. The counter argument coming from the neoliberal AfT camp is that trade may help generate economic growth, but trade alone is not adequate to achieve economic growth.

Notwithstanding that both AfT and TnA concepts may be understood to be embedded in neoliberal ideologies as defined by the Washington Consensus, Trump seems to be shifting the development aid focus towards a mercantilist ideology. That is, Trump is stepping back from globalisation and is embracing mercantilist trade policies with strong predilections for bilateral deals. This is poised to have unintentional consequences for development aid, especially if the Trump administration links foreign trade and development aid. One of these consequences is Trump's potential retreat from the accepted policies and practices of free trade and their replacement with Trumponomics-based fair-trade policies, which he defines in mercantilist and TnA terms. By rejecting the conventional understanding of the fair-trade concept (see Anderson 2013) and replacing it with a mercantilist notion of fair-trade, Trump is setting a scene for zero-sum trade arrangement. This means that by shifting from AfT to TnA, USA foreign trade and development aid provides opportunities for the USA to achieve economic advantages at the expense of others.

This does not necessarily mean that Trump will abandon AfT development aid altogether, but that the USA will leverage its aid budget and contributions to IFIs to obtain more favourable trade deals. How such leverage may be pursued and implemented remains open to interpretation. It may be that the USA withholds development aid to certain developing countries unless they reduce tariffs for USA goods and services. Or the Trump administration might limit development aid to countries that require aid but do not have sufficient trade to leverage, leading to a partial implementation of TnA policies.

Scenario: Trumponomics and the Development Aid Diplomacy

The USA's disengagement from certain world affairs based on the Trump 'America First' doctrine is setting the direction of the Trump administration development aid diplomacy. To recall, over the past 70 years, namely since the advent of the Truman Doctrine, development aid remained an important component of foreign policy. The new 'America First' doctrine is setting a scenario for replacing the Truman Doctrine, thus transforming the post-Cold War order and the neoliberal dominated development aid. Consequently, the 'America First' doctrine may achieve the opposite of what is intended: it could diminish the USA's geopolitical, geo-economic and global economic leadership. There are two issues to be considered: (i) the Trump administration is proposing a significant cut to the development aid budget; (ii) Trump has categorically stated that his administration will conduct a foreign policy focussing on USA economic and political interests, which is based on a vision of national security. The Trump administration is starting to implement this policy as evidenced by a reduction of about USD 100 million in economic and military aid to Egypt (Gallo 2017) and has suspended USD 300 million in aid previously pledged to compensate Pakistan for counterterrorism campaigns (McLeary and De Luce (2017).

Regarding the budget cut, the Trump administration has, for the 2018 fiscal year, proposed an international affairs budget of USD 37.6 billion. This amounts to a reduction of the State Department and USAID budget of between 31% (see MacArthur 2017) and 37% (see Schwartz 2017) compared to the 2017 fiscal year. However, the proposal has not received much support from the Republican dominated Congress, putting Trump's foreign aid budget agenda into question. The Republican Senate sub-committee chairperson responsible for diplomacy and foreign aid spending, rejected the proposed cuts because it would diminish USA's soft power abilities and global impact significantly (Torbati 2017). The argument against the budget cut is that the USA would be forced to withdraw from its global leadership role and suffer a decline in geopolitical and geo-economic influences. Some members of the USA Congress and the Senate are opposing the cuts, while others are arguing that the cuts are not big enough. There are even some Republican conservative voices who argue against funding development aid altogether; the latter would be the worst-case scenario, and the former (i.e. the rejection of budget cuts) the best-case scenario.

However speculative, perhaps the most likely scenario will be a reduction to the development aid budget as well as USA's contributions to Bretton Woods institutions and other IFIs, which may be smaller than that proposed by the Trump administration. If this scenario became reality, the Trump administration would, intentionally or otherwise, weaken the social and political principles, values and norms, and its global leadership which it maintained since the end of WWII. It would also undermine its own interests as articulated by Trump, namely safeguarding global respect for the USA through a projection of economic and military power and dominance, and the pursuit of diplomacy with new friends and allies, and old enemies. However, to achieve this Trump's strategy is based on bilateral, rather than multilateral, negotiations and diplomacy and a mercantilist zero-sum game where the USA must be the sole beneficiary. There is not much room for soft power diplomacy, rather the embracement of hard power diplomacy.

The term 'soft power' was coined by Nye (1991, 2004) and defined as a country's capability to convince another country or institution to follow its wishes without coercion or force. The concept is generally used as foreign policy diplomacy using social, cultural, political and economic means. To clarify, in contrast to soft power diplomacy, hard power diplomacy denotes a scenario when a nation enforces its will on other nations through military, economic or geopolitical strategies. The USA has, over the past decades and especially since the end of the Cold War, evolved from a strong leaning towards hard power to soft power diplomacy. However, this seems to be changing under the Trump administration. As Mick Mulvaney, Trump administration Budget Director reportedly stated, "… the proposed budget reflects the government's priorities"—thus hard power diplomacy is being used over soft power diplomacy to boost the USA's military power (see Westwood 2017). The potential outcome of the shift towards hard power policies at expense of soft power diplomacy is that the Trump administration will forego the benefits of the diplomatic investments in soft power underpinned by development aid.

Retreating from soft power diplomacy and moving towards hard power military activities, as advocated by the Trump administration snubs not only the USA foreign policy since the Marshall Plan, but also neglects the importance and necessity of soft power politics and diplomacy, including development aid. It appears that for the Trump administration only one scenario is emerging: abolish soft power diplomacy and establish hard power diplomacy.

The above-stated development aid budget cut deliberately moves the Trump administration away from soft power diplomacy and is a catalyst for ideological change in USA development aid. This ideology points towards a foreign policy where military action is the dominant mechanism for solving international problems. The determination to focus USA's foreign policy strategies on defence and reduce the foundations of diplomacy and development aid will inescapably create unintended impacts for the Trump administration foreign policies. Once the USA reduces its funding for development aid it may neither be able to maintain its currently dominant global role and influence nor will it be able to re-establish its current global political leadership in multilateral cooperation, especially concerning security issues beyond military challenges. This will lead to the rise of asymmetrical foreign relations and reduce the options available to the USA in preventing future global or regional conflicts.

To conclude, since the end of WWII the USA established and maintained its position as the development aid superpower. It has been, and still is, the single largest development aid donor and contributor to IFIs, UNDP and other UN aid programs. However, the emerging rejection of soft power diplomacy and the aim to strengthen hard power diplomacy, combined with an increased focus on domestic economic development at the expense of foreign aid, the USA under the Trump administration will not be able to fully align its development aid policies with those of other Western democratic governments. The USA's shift from soft to hard power diplomacy will, out of necessity, push developing countries to find alternative development aid with other donors, such as China-led New Development Bank (NDB), Asian Infrastructure Investment Bank (AIIB) and the One Belt One Road (OBOR) initiative, and the European Bank for Reconstruction and Development, to name but a few. The USA, under the Trump administration, may well become a development aid niche player rather than a global leader.

Scenario: Trumponomics, the Beijing Consensus and the Future of Development Aid

Prior to proceeding with the discussion concerning the future of development aid within a framework of Trumponomics and the Beijing Consensus, it may be opportune to unpack the latter. Williamson (2012) defines the Beijing Consensus in the broadest terms as an economic development paradigm. The term was coined by Ramo (2004, p. 4) who describes it as:

> China's new development approach [which] is driven by a desire to have equitable, peaceful high-quality growth, critically speaking, it turns traditional ideas like privatisation and free trade on their heads. It is flexible enough that it is barely classifiable as a doctrine. It does not believe in uniform solutions for every situation. It is defined by a ruthless willingness to innovate and experiment, by a lively defence of national borders and interests, and by the increasingly thoughtful accumulation of tools of asymmetric power projection. It is pragmatic and ideological at the same time, a reflection of an ancient Chinese philosophical outlook that makes little distinction between theory and practice.

The Beijing Consensus, according to Ramo, rejects the neoliberal economic theory of the Washington Consensus, with its one size-fits-all doctrine and it rejects Fukuyama's 'End of History' proposition. In addition to focussing on economic change, it equally considers social changes and utilises economics and governance to advance societal needs (Ramo 2004). In short, the Beijing Consensus highlights a number of socio-economic and socio-political thoughts which emerged in China in opposition to the Thatcherism and Reaganism neoliberal ideologies that are still dominating the development aid agenda of the IFIs.

The point of departure for this scenario is that both Trumponomics and the Beijing Consensus will have a significant impact on the future of development aid. The Trump administration is pursuing a policy of USA's disengagement from the Washington Consensus-based development aid and potentially scaling back its support for the Bretton Woods and similar multilateral institutions. In contrast, China is pursuing development aid policies with increased involvement in global development aid based on the principles of the Beijing Consensus.

If this stands to reason, it could be argued that due to Trumponomics the Washington Consensus is in descent and the China's Beijing Consensus is in ascent. Thus, Trumponomics and China's foreign aid and development policies are not in competition; both are independent of each other and both are putting the neoliberal Washington Consensus on notice.

The most likely scenario is that the Trump administration, will by the virtue of its own resolve, retreat from a leadership role in the global development arena and China will extend its sphere of influence through soft power diplomacy and the Beijing Consensus. The discussion of a number of questions may provide an understanding of the future of development aid in the context of Trumponomics and the Beijing Consensus. For example, will China step forward and take on the mantra of development aid global leadership, a position vacated by the USA under the Trump administration? On basis of the current Chinese foreign policies, the

Scenario: Trumponomics, the Beijing Consensus and the Future ...

answer is yes. The second question is: if China takes on the role of leadership, what impact will this have on development aid? There are two interrelated aspects to this question: one concerns the impact of the ascent of China as a global leader in development aid, and the other concerns the impact of the combined descent of the USA as a global leader in development aid the neoliberal development aid agenda. This is underpinned by the USA budget cuts scenario and the pursuit of a hard power foreign policy.

Let us now turn to China's attempts to take on the mantra of development aid global leadership, from which the USA under the Trump administration is retreating. China's preparedness to take global leadership in the development aid arena is obvious. China has established and is leading the AIIB, has taken a prominent role in the formation of the NDB and is the leader in the OBOR initiative. This puts China on a trajectory to become the largest asymmetric economic super power using soft power diplomacy based on the Beijing Consensus as one of the strategies to achieve its global domination. This is in stark contrast to the emerging USA style hard power diplomacy approach and the demise of the soft power foreign policies and tools of development aid. Furthermore, China is building its emerging economic global leadership foundation and development aid strategies based on its own economic model. This includes the tolerance of the Westphalian system of national sovereignty of aid recipient countries—a blunt rejection of the economic neoliberal prescriptiveness of the Washington Consensus.

Given the scenario that the USA under the Trump administration is stepping back from its global leadership role in development aid, and China, together with its Asian allies, is redesigning the international development aid landscape in Asia and Africa, China is showing overtly its readiness to take on the global leadership role. A role which is increasingly been vacated by the Trump administration. There are signs that China's ascent to global dominance in the development aid arena will impact on or even marginalise the Bretton Woods institutions, and other IFIs which follow the Washington Consensus (see Jakupec and Kelly 2015).

We can now turn to the second question, namely if China takes on the role of leadership, what impact will this have on development aid? The two interrelated concerns are: (i) the impact of the ascent of China as a global leader in development aid on the USA and development aid countries, and (ii) the impact of USA descent as a global leader in development aid and the neoliberal development aid agenda.

The Beijing Consensus poses several problems and challenges for the USA. One problem for Trump's USA is that China will use its soft power initiative together with the leverage of the AIIB, the NDB, the OBOR initiative and its own development aid assistance based on the Beijing Consensus, as a catalyst for advancing its geopolitical ascent. It can thereby secure, expand and strengthen its political and economic sphere of influence. Furthermore, the USA's dominance of the World Bank, IMF and WTO, and its significant influence in a number of regional development banks, such as the ADB, together with the Trump administration's threat to reduce funding commitments, would steer these IFIs towards a mercantilist development aid model, leaving a substantial gap for the China-led development banks and initiatives to fill. This scenario questions the future domination of the Bretton Woods system and the neoliberal Washington Consensus.

There are indications that few of the current players—the World Bank, the IMF, multilateral aid agencies, such as the ADB, and USA bilateral aid agencies, such as the USAID and MCC—adequately recognise the emergence and impact of the rising economies in the developing world. These are often economies that do not wish to embrace the Washington Consensus aid conditionalities, such as the neoliberal principals of privatisation, reduction of trade barriers and tariffs and others. The issue is that the USA maintains veto rights and may direct the flow of development aid funding according to its own development aid policies.

There is, of course, the potential scenario that the USA will become a member country and contributor to the AIIB, NDB and the OBOR initiative, and thus it will be able to influence the direction that these institutions and initiatives may take. For various reasons this is highly improbable. China is not likely to step back from its leadership role in the OBOR project, AIIB and the NDB. It should be noted that the USA, together with Japan and very few other countries, have not joined the AIIB, nor is it part of NDB.

Setting the scenario for the USA losing its global leadership in the development aid arena two factors arise. One is China's soft power initiative, and the other is the Beijing Consensus. To restate, 'soft power' as defined by Nye (2004) includes a nation's social, cultural, economic and political values, foreign policies and economic attractions. These are denoted as national strengths and as instruments of persuasion for other countries to willingly (i.e. without political coercion, economic pressures or military interventions) accept the same values, policies and attractions.

Notwithstanding that China's culture has prevailed for millenniums on the Asian continent, it was unable to compete with the Western cultural values emanating from the USA in the mid-20th century. Yet, in the late 20th century and despite USA dominance, China has adopted its own pragmatic approach to development aid and developed its own economic development paradigm known as the Beijing Consensus (Williamson 2012). China's approach is based on a soft power policy with the central notion of non-interference in domestic affairs of developing countries. It counters the Western democracies' concepts of neoliberal economic reforms and political liberalisation.

It is noteworthy that China has over the last decade successfully exported its economic development model to developing nations in Asia and Africa. The main strength of China as a major donor in the development aid arena is that it encourages the development aid recipient countries to develop and pursue their own economic development through trade and investment into social institutions, programs and infrastructure. The Beijing Consensus does not impose the political and economic reform conditionalities of the Washington Consensus.

It could be argued that a retreat by the Trump administration from development aid leadership will reduce its funding to IFIs. Together with the unpalatability of the Washington Consensus neoliberal aid conditionalities, and the USA mercantilist TnA policies, developing countries will look for alternative sources of development aid funding. They will turn away from the USA's Trumponomics and the neoliberal model of development aid of the IFIs. Losing the geopolitical and geo-economic sphere of interests in developing countries will most likely undercut the hegemonic status of the USA.

Conclusion

As noted above, the neoliberal development aid agenda is coming under attack from two sides. One is from the populist movement, especially Trumponomics, and the other is China's Beijing Consensus. These attacks have the potential to render the Bretton Woods, and other development aid agencies which follow the neoliberal Washington Consensus, increasingly less relevant. Furthermore, the Washington Consensus institutions such as the World Bank, IMF, WTO, and other regional development banks have neither show an interest in understanding the impact of the Beijing Consensus, nor have they adequately responded to the challenges that it poses to the neoliberal development aid agenda.

As Davies and Howes (2017) observed:

> With China's rapid economic progress, the Beijing Consensus is in the ascendency. Trump's presidency is likely to accelerate this trend. First, his election and the deep divides in American society that it has revealed seem to cast further doubt on the pro-market policies and democratic values traditionally championed by the United States. Second, Trump's mercantilism and his professed admiration of authoritarian leaders seem to validate key aspects of the Beijing Consensus. It is early days, but the greatest developmental impact of the Trump presidency may be to cement the Beijing Consensus as the pre-eminent global development model (n.p.).

The basic political vantage point taken by the Trump administration in relation to foreign policies, including development aid, is to ensure USA's economic prosperity, the maintenance of social values and physical security. This has been the USA's approach for over two centuries. The difference between the approach taken by previous USA administrations and the Trump administration is Trump's personal world view concerning the characteristics of the international geopolitical and geo-economic environment, and how this environment threatens the USA economy, security and its way of life. For Trump, the main threats appear to be the powerful external forces of neoliberal globalisation, which resonates directly with the USA domestic arena and the economically disadvantaged population.

Trumponomics repudiates the claims that neoliberalism has won the ideological political contest and there was nothing else to challenge it. There was, of course, no 'End of History', only a shift in ideologies. That is, as discussed in previous chapters, Fukuyama's notion of the 'End of History' was an argument in favour of the end of ideology akin to the discourse in the works of Friedrich Hegel and Daniel Bell. Fukuyama's proclamation remained mainly unchallenged, but only for a short time. The ideological challenge to the neoliberal project, which rose with Thatcherism and Reaganomics and continued in modified versions, in the Western political and economic arenas came from an unsuspected quarter, namely the rise of populism.

Populism cautions against the neoliberal policies by claiming that these have socially, politically and economically run their course with a result that has provided many benefits for the elite, establishment and multinational corporations, and little for the domestic working and middle-class population. It is important to recall that populism is an anti-neoliberal economic movement, as well as a nativist and nationalist movement. This is also reflected in the populist policies concerning development aid and a hostility towards cosmopolitanism, globalisation, especially the Washington Consensus, and the ideologies of the Bretton Woods institutions.

So, will the populist movement change development aid as it is practised by the Washington Consensus institutions and other like-minded IFIs? The answer is most likely in the affirmative. There are a number of reasons for this proposition. Firstly, given that the USA as the single largest global contributor to development aid is reducing its involvement and abolishing its leadership role in the global development aid arena, and given the potential for other countries, such as the UK, to follow suit due to domestic pressure, development aid funding and conditions may change.

Against the above background, the question is: what are the challenges concerning development aid at a crossroad between the Washington Consensus and neoliberal globalisation, national populism and the Beijing Consensus? The point that should be made here is that the Washington Consensus has a coherent theoretical framework based on neoliberalism. Trumponomics, on the other hand, is couched in mercantilism. Thus both, the Washington Consensus and Trumponomics, in contrast to the Beijing Consensus have a theoretical grounding. In short, to re-emphasise the Beijing Consensus lacks a theoretical foundation. This constellation makes it difficult to articulate a coherent argument delineating the direction of development aid, or to project the impact of Trump's populism. Nevertheless, China with its Beijing Consensus-based development aid seems to be increasingly succeeding in extending its geopolitical influence in Asia and Africa. In contrast to the USA, China portrays itself as a stable and steady development donor. On the other hand, USA under the Trump administration is being increasingly perceived as unpredictable, which is struggling to define its development aid polices and the Washington Consensus.

Trump's populist attack on development aid is based on his perception of the weaknesses of the IFIs and the failure to protect the interests and values of the USA. Thus, Trumponomics is a reaction against the global neoliberalism and, as such, it has a strong destabilising impact on the Washington Consensus based development aid. Will the Bretton Woods institutions and other IFIs that follow the neoliberal ideology be able to withstand the Trump administration attacks without disruption to their funding levels and continuity? There is no simple answer. The complexity of a response to this question emerges from two factors. Firstly, the World Bank, the IMF, the WTO and other multilateral IFIs have shown limited ability and willingness to move beyond the Washington Consensus conditionalities. Secondly, China and its Beijing Consensus together with the AIIB, the NDB and the OBOR initiative, now successfully competes with the Bretton Woods and other IFIs, without demanding economic, political or social conditionalities from recipient countries.

Conclusion 83

Trump's mercantilism manifesting in proposed funding cuts to development aid the Washington Consensus institutions, together with the rise of China's Beijing Consensus institutions and initiatives, is creating an existential relevance breaking point for the IFIs. Both USA and China are independently challenging the existing IFIs neoliberal orthodoxies. While Trump seeks to dismantle neoliberal globalisation as far as development aid is concerned, China is stepping back from the imposition of neoliberal development aid conditionality. Taking into consideration the rise of populism in the USA and the rise of China as a dominant development aid global player, it is not too difficult to imagine that the neoliberal epoch in the development aid arena has had its day. Both China and USA will try to define it in a new context. It may be useful to rethink the whole idea of neoliberalism as it relates to development aid. As we contemplate the approaching end of the Fukuyamian 'End of History' epoch, perhaps we should try to comprehend populism not as an economic, social or political bogyman, but as a catalyst for new political [dis-] order.

The rise of populism movements, especially on the right, are foreshadowing significant structural changes in the development aid arena. It is unlikely that these changes will be arrested or even reversed any time soon. Thus, it would be difficult to argue that right-wing populism will fade away in the foreseeable future. Furthermore, populist parties and movements in the development aid donor countries with their anti-establishment sentiments are gaining influence, whilst the major established neoliberal parties are losing their political hold on power. Thus, the rise of right-wing populism casts begs the question whether development aid donor nations will maintain their commitment to their development aid agenda. Will the USA under 'America First' doctrine, the UK post-Brexit, the EU with the demands from the 'Visegrád Four' plus far-right Austria, and others continue to provide ODA funding for reducing poverty in developing countries, or will such funding be redirected to their domestic budget and own population? Most likely, it will not be an either-or scenario, the most likely outcome will be that under right wing populist agendas, development aid funding will be reduced and new conditionalities accompanying development aid allocation will emerge.

References

ADB (Asian Development Bank). 2017. *Annual Report 2016*. Manila: ADB.

Alderman, L. 2017. Macron vowed to be business friendly. Now he faces a protectionist uproar. *New York Times*. https://www.nytimes.com/2017/08/01/business/france-macron-jobs-economy.html?emc=edit_mbe_20170802&nl=morning-briefing-europe&nlid=77462579&te=1. Accessed on August 1, 2017.

Anderson, M. 2013. Fair trade: Partnership in development? A reassessment of trading partnerships with the fair trade model. In *The Processes and Practices of Fair Trade: Trust, Ethics and Governance*, eds. B. Granville and J. Janet Dine. Milton Park and New York: Routledge.

Bello, W. 2002. *Deglobalization: Ideas for a New World Economy*. New York: Zed Books.

Bello, W. 2013. *Capitalism's Last Stand?*. London: Zed Books.

Bouman, M. 2017. Geert Wilders and Donald Trump can learn from Marine Le Print. *Dutch News*. http://www.dutchnews.nl/features/2017/02/geert-wilders-and-donald-trump-can-learn-from-marine-le-print/. Accessed April 17, 2017.

Davies, R., and S. Howes. 2017. Trump and development: Aid, migration and the Beijing Consensus. *ANU College of Asia & The Pacific*. http://asiapacific.anu.edu.au/trump-100-days/trump-and-development-aid-migration-and-beijing-consensus. Accessed August 11, 2107.

Dorsey, T. 2007. *What is Aid for Trade?*. Washington, DC: IMF Policy Development and Review Department.

Easterly, W. 2006a. *The White Man's Burden: Why the West's Efforts to Aid the Rest Have Done So Much Ill and So Little Good*. Oxford: Oxford University Press.

Easterly, W. 2006b. Why doesn't aid work? *Cato Unbound*. http://www.cato-unbound.org/2006/04/03/william-easterly/why-doesnt-aid-work/. Accessed April 6, 2017.

Easterly, W. 2008. Design and reform of institutions in LDCs and transition economies institutions: Top down or bottom up? *American Economic Review* 98 (2): 95–99.

Gallagher, K.P. 2011. China challenges Washington's 'trade-no-aid' strategy in Latin America. *East Asia Forum*. http://www.eastasiaforum.org/2011/03/19/china-challenges-washingtons-trade-not-aid-strategy-in-latin-america/. Accessed August 2, 2017.

Gallo, W. 2017. US withholds aid from Egypt over rights concerns. *VOA*. https://www.voanews.com/a/us-aid-egypt-kushner/3997081.html. Accessed September 8, 2017.

Goldin, I., and K. Reinert. 2007. *Globalization for Development: Trade, Finance, Aid, Migration, and Policy*. New York: The World Bank and Palgrave Macmillan.

Goodhart, D. 2017. *The Road to Somewhere: The Populist Revolt and the Future of Politics*. London: Hurst & Company.

Gun, D., C. Keller, S. Kochugovindan, and T. Wieladek. 2017. The end of globalisation as we know it? *Barclay Insights*. https://www.investmentbank.barclays.com/our-insights/the-end-of-globalisation-as-we-know-it.html. Accessed August 2, 2017.

IMF (International Monetary Fund). 2017. IMF Members' Quotas and Voting Power, and IMF Board of Governors. *IMF*. https://www.imf.org/external/np/sec/memdir/members.aspx. Accessed August 7, 2017.

Jakupec, V., and M. Kelly. 2015. The relevance of Asian development bank: Existing in the shadow of the Asian infrastructure investment bank. *Journal of Regional Socio-Economic Issues* 5 (3): 31–46.

King, S.D. 2017. *Grave New World: The End of Globalization, the Return of History*. New Haven and London: Yale University Press.

MacArthur, J. 2017. Congressional leaders voice concern about Trump administration's proposed cuts to state department and USAID. *Modernising Foreign Assistance Network*. http://modernizeaid.net/2017/03/congressional-leaders-voice-concern-trump-administrations-proposed-cuts-state-department-usaid/. Accessed April 7, 2017.

McLeary, P., and D. De Luce. 2017. Trump administration threatens to cut aid to Pakistan. Does it matter? *Foreign Policy*. http://foreignpolicy.com/2017/08/23/trump-administration-threatens-to-cut-aid-to-pakistan-does-it-matter/. Accessed September 8, 2017.

Negin, J. 2014. *Understanding Aid for Trade Part One: A Dummy's Guide*. Canberra: Development Policy Centre, Australian National University.

Nye, J.S. 1991. *Bound to Lead: The Challenging Nature of American Power*. New York: Basic Books.

Nye, J.S. 2004. *Soft Power: The Means to Success in World Politics*. New York: Public Affairs.

Ramo, J.C. 2004. *The Beijing Consensus*. London: Foreign Policy Centre.

Ranaweera, T. 2003. *Foreign Aid, Conditionality, and Ghost of the Financing Gap: A Forgotten Aspect of the Aid Debate*. World Bank Policy Research Working Paper 3019. Washington DC: World Bank.

Sachs, J.D. 2005a. *The End of Poverty: Economic Possibilities for Our Time*. New York: The Penguin Press.

References 85

Sachs, J.D. 2005b. *The End of Poverty: How We Can Make It Happen in Our Lifetime*. London: Penguin.

Sachs, J.D., and J.W. McArthur. 2005. The millennium project: A plan for meeting the millennium development goals. *The Lancet* 365 (9456): 347–353.

Schwartz, F. 2017. Trump proposes cutting state department budget by 37%. *The Wall Street Journal*. https://www.wsj.com/articles/white-house-proposes-cutting-state-department-budget-by-one-third-1488306999. Accessed April 28, 2017.

Swarup, B. 2016. Deglobalisation 2.0. *Terra Firma* (15 August 2016). https://www.terrafirma.com/an-alternative-perspective-article/items/deglobalisation-20.html. Accessed October 11, 2017.

Therborn, G. 2000. Globalisations: Dimensions, historical waves, religious effects. *Normative Governance. International Sociology* 15 (2): 151–179.

Torbati, Y. 2017. Republicans push back against Trump plan to cut foreign aid. *Reuters Business News*. http://www.reuters.com/article/us-usa-budget-foreign-aid-idUSKBN18J2DC. Accessed August 8, 2017.

Westwood, S. 2017. Trump's 'soft power' budget cuts draw hard opposition. *Washington Examiner*. http://www.washingtonexaminer.com/trumps-soft-power-budget-cuts-draw-hard-opposition/article/2618259. Accessed August 10, 2017.

Williamson, J. 2012. Is the "Beijing Consensus" now dominant? *Asia Policy* 13: 1–16.

World Bank. 2017. IBRD subscriptions and voting power of member countries. *IBRD*. https://finances.worldbank.org/Shareholder-Equity/IBRD-Subscriptions-and-Voting-Power-of-Member-Coun/rcx4-r7xj/data. Accessed August 6, 2017.

WTO. 2015a. Development: Aid for trade: Factsheet. *WTO*. https://www.wto.org/English/Tratop_E/devel_e/a4t_e/a4t_factsheet_e.htm). Accessed February 12, 2017.

WTO. 2015b. Development: Aid for trade. *WTO*. https://www.wto.org/english/tratop_e/devel_e/a4t_e/aid4trade_e.htm. Accessed February 12, 2017.

Manufactured by Amazon.ca
Bolton, ON